Whitman
Publishing, LLC

MORGAN DOLLAR

Legendary Coins and the Making of the Modern Market
Featuring the Coins of the Coronet Collection

Michael "Miles" Standish
With Reminiscences by John B. Love
Foreword by John M. Mercanti

Whitman Publishing, LLC
PUBLISHING SINCE 1934
www.whitman.com

MORGAN DOLLAR
Legendary Coins and the Making of the Modern Market

www.whitman.com

© 2014 Whitman Publishing, LLC
3101 Clairmont Road · Suite G
Atlanta, GA 30329

ISBN: 0794842771
Printed in the United States of America

Disclaimer: No warranty or representation of any kind is made concerning the accuracy or completeness of the information presented, or its usefulness in purchases or sales. The opinions of others may vary. The author and consultants may buy, sell, and sometimes hold certain of the items discussed in this book.

Caveat: This book is designed to provide accurate and authoritative information with regard to the subject matters covered. It is distributed with the understanding that Whitman Publishing and the author are not engaged in rendering legal, financial, or other professional services. If expert professional assistance is required, the services of a competent professional should be sought. The guidance herein is subject to differences of opinion. Before making decisions to buy or sell numismatic collectibles, consult the latest information, including current market conditions. Past performance of the rare-coin market, or any coin or series within that market, is not necessarily an indication of future performance, as the future is unknown. Such factors as changing demand, popularity, grading interpretations, strength of the overall market, and national and international economic conditions will continue to be influences.

Whitman Publishing is a leader in the antiques and collectibles field. For a catalog of related books, supplies, and storage products, visit Whitman Publishing online at **Whitman.com**.

Contents

Acknowledgements

The author would like to thank all the great, fine people who graded, traded, shared their knowledge, and played a role in growing the popularity of the Morgan dollar series, including the following: Bruce Amspacher, Dick Armstrong, Joe Bachagloupe, Michael Berkman, Kent Brennan, Ryan Carroll, Steve Contursi, Adam Crum, James Curtis, Mike De Falco, Kenneth Duncan, Michael Fuljenz, Bill Gale, David Hall, Leon Hendrickson, David Hendrickson, Dean Heskin, Scott Hocevar, Ron Howard, Gordon Jankowski, Keith Kelman, John Levy, Kevin Lipton, Joe Mangione, Steve Mayer, Carl Melillo, Wayde Milas, Jordan Miller, Wayne Miller, Rick Montgomery, Charles Morgan, Edgar Nobel, Thad Olson, Ted Robinson, Mike Sargent, Van Simmons, Craig Smith, William Spears, Eric Streiner, Karl Tackett, and Hubert Walker.

Also, this book would not have been possible without the love and support of Burdell M. and Marie T. Standish, who allowed me to pursue all of my dreams and desires in life. Thank you both.

A quick anecdote: My grandfather Harold Standish opened up "Stan's" Snack Shop in the small town of Augusta, Michigan, which is located just a few miles from Fort Custer. In the 1940s, Stan's was the place to stop for a quality hamburger, and you could top it off with a scoop of my dad's delicious homemade ice cream. Harold would often pull coins from the register that he liked to put in his collection. Sometimes he would find Standing Liberty quarters, Morgan dollars, and everything in between. My dad even caught the collecting bug and once had the great fortune of finding an elusive Three-Legged Buffalo nickel on the floor one night while sweeping up. This is where the Standish family got its start collecting coins.

Whitman Publishing would like to thank John M. Mercanti, former chief engraver of the U.S. Mint, for writing the foreword to this book. PCGS shared photographs of the Coronet Collection of Morgan dollars, pictured in chapter 4. Charles Morgan and Hubert Walker assisted with the text manuscript. John Love was interviewed for his recollections and observations on the Morgan dollar market. Blanche Bowers reviewed the manuscript. The Library of Congress provided certain historical images for chapter 1. Various historical coin images are used, with permission, from the *Guide Book of United States Coins* (the "Red Book," by R.S. Yeoman, edited by Kenneth Bressett). Paper-money images in chapter 1 are from the *Encyclopedia of U.S. Paper Money* (by Q. David Bowers).

I first met Miles Standish six or seven years ago at a Whitman Coin & Collectibles Expo in Philadelphia. Prior to that we spoke over the phone a number of times, discussing my post-retirement plans, but had not met in person.

I was at the show seated at a concession booth with a number of my friends and two or three of my engraving staff who attended the show with me when I looked up and saw this gentleman looking at me with a huge infectious smile—a grin that went from ear to ear—and wearing a shirt that clearly announced "I'm from Texas."

That day changed my life. Since then I've accomplished things I never thought I'd be able to do. I've coauthored with Miles a book that became a bestseller in our field (*American Silver Eagles: A Guide to the U.S. Bullion Coin Program*), and I've designed and sculpted a coin for the Perth Mint in Australia. And it's all been made possible by that grinning Texan.

In this book Miles discusses, evaluates, and educates the reader on one of America's most beautiful coins, the Morgan silver dollar. The reader will learn about the pace of the nation in the era of the Morgan dollar. . . what precipitated the need for a new dollar coin. . . the design process. . . and more, including photos and references showing variations and types.

As a coin designer I was extremely interested in the chapter on the design of the dollar. You'll learn about the friction between William Barber and George Morgan—a precursor to the feud between his son Charles and Augustus Saint-Gaudens over the design of the gold eagles. This brought to mind a story that Frank Gasparro told me. It seems that when he first came to the U.S. Mint in the capacity of an engraver, John Sinnock did not at all like him. He felt that Frank had used his influence to get the position and wasn't fully qualified. In fact, he banished Frank to a room off to the side and away from the engraving staff, where he worked alone for a number of months. I don't think Frank ever forgave him for that. Artists, sculptors, and engravers can be very sensitive, volatile, and possessive about their designs. I know

U.S. Mint chief engraver John Mercanti inspecting a new ten-cent die at the Philadelphia Mint, February 25, 2010. (Andrew Harrer / Bloomberg via Getty Images)

John M. Mercanti (right) and Edmund C. Moy (38th director of the U.S. Mint) at the Whitman Coin & Collectibles Baltimore Expo, November 8, 2013. Mercanti holds the second edition of his award-winning book, *American Silver Eagles*.

this from experience. Many times in my career I've had to separate members of my staff over design disputes or send someone home to cool off. To some degree I can sympathize with the Barbers. They had the responsibility of designing and producing United States currency, but they weren't open to change.

When Morgan was instructed to create models for his dollar, he probably worked in red wax. Three of these wax models still exist, although they are not of the Morgan dollar. They are magnificent pieces of artwork, and it's my hope that someday they will be on display along with the hundred or so patterns the Mint has. I've seen, in the Mint vault, patterns that resemble the Morgan dollar. They may have been preliminary models but we had no documentation.

I predict that this book will be the "go to" book on the Morgan dollar. It's informative, easy to read, and perfect for the experienced Morgan collector or for the new collector just starting out, and it is written by the best grader in the industry—that grinning Texan, Miles Standish.

Enjoy your journey.

John M. Mercanti
12th Chief Engraver
United States Mint

John M. Mercanti is an American sculptor and engraver, best known to numismatists as the 12th chief engraver of the U.S. Mint and the designer of many circulating and commemorative coins and medals.

Mercanti was born in Philadelphia. It was there that he received his artistic training, at the Pennsylvania Academy of Fine Arts, the Philadelphia College of Art, and the Fleisher Art Memorial School. He began his career as an illustrator and in 1974 joined the U.S. Mint as a sculptor-engraver under the legendary Frank Gasparro. In 2006 Mercanti was named chief engraver (supervisory design and master tooling development specialist), a position he held until his retirement in late 2010.

John Mercanti has produced more coin and medal designs than any other employee in the history of the U.S. Mint. Among his works (in addition to the reverse of the American Silver Eagle) are gold and silver commemorative coins honoring the Statue of Liberty, the Olympic Games, Dwight Eisenhower, the Smithsonian Institution, and other important people, places, and events from American history; more than a dozen Congressional Gold Medals; five circulating State quarters; and numerous commemorative and bullion medals.

His book *American Silver Eagles: A Guide to the U.S. Bullion Coin Program* won an "Extraordinary Merit" award from the Numismatic Literary Guild.

Mercanti resides in New Jersey, across the Delaware River and not far from his workplace of nearly 40 years, the Philadelphia Mint.

MORGAN DOLLAR

Legendary Coins and the Making of the Modern Market

Chapter One

America of the Morgan Dollar Era

The great coins tell a story.

They engage us. They fascinate us. They beckon us to dig deep into the past so we can relate to the aspirations, the struggles, and the achievements of the people for whom they were created. They are totems that connect us to who we once were.

Coins belong not only to the past and the present, but also, if we're careful, to the future. As they pass through our hands, we become subtle footnotes to their stories.

Colonial coppers, for example, remind us of the dreams and desires of pioneering generations of European immigrants who fled the despotism of an old world to begin anew. The coins were born out of necessity and revealed to the colonists just what a tenuous hold the European powers had on the New World. They were one of the opening salvos in support of American independence.

Early federal coinage, with its designs and symbols, shows us a country that eschewed the trappings of nobility in favor of the idealization of Liberty. Our fledgling nation revealed itself in the motifs and mottos used on our coins: coins that not only facilitated trade within the borders of this country but also served as ambassadors for the United States and its people abroad.

Rosa Americana 1723 Penny

1792 Birch Cent

Penny (Denarium)

High-Relief Head

1795 half dollar

Draped Bust dollar

Penny (Denarium)

St. Patrick "Halfpenny"

1795 eagle

Morgan dollar

So how does the story of the Morgan dollar fit into this pageant of American life? Numismatists have been trying to answer that question for many years. Some blame it for leading the country into financial ruin at the end of the 19th century, yet it also saved an empire at the beginning of the 20th. The Morgan dollar is just as important for its shortcomings as it is for its triumphs.

Once so common that almost no one thought it would ever be a great collectible, the Morgan dollar was propelled into the limelight by the collapse in value of its most coveted issues in 1962, bringing unprecedented enthusiasm to the series and to numismatics in general. The Morgan dollar is now, as it's always been, a coin of contradictions.

As collectors, we enjoy the sheer heft, the size, the look, and the color of a coin in hand. But to focus solely on the coin's physical properties, the way in which it was produced, the players who made it all possible—not to mention how effective it was as a circulating medium—is to miss the point. The richness of the Morgan dollar takes each of these things into account, for sure, but its value stems from so much more than that. In order to truly appreciate the Morgan dollar—to understand its strange life—we should first acquaint ourselves with the America of the Morgan dollar era.

Here, then, is some of its story.

A History Not So Distant....

The country that ushered in the Morgan dollar in 1878 was a much different place than it is now. Great matters of national significance remained unsettled. The America of the 20th century was busy being born.

The psychic and material wounds of the Civil War were still fresh. A whole generation of sons had been wiped out by a war that claimed more than 620,000 men. To put that number in context, it would take the combined U.S. military actions of both world wars, Korea, and Vietnam before our nation would suffer such a loss in human lives.

Much work remained in terms of the United States' territorial aspirations. Vast expanses of the country's western interior were still wild. Large swaths were unsettled, and law and order were secured only through the barrel of a gun. When the first Morgan dollars left the San Francisco and Carson City mints in 1878, the Union consisted of 38 states. By the time the last pieces were struck in 1921, the wild western regions of the country had been carved up and parceled out for a continent-spanning total of 48.

In the South, the policy of Reconstruction had come to an abrupt, politically expedient close—the actual rebuilding of Southern communities would be a long process. However, the reinstitution of anti-black laws was almost immediate. Through intimidation and the perversion of law, freed men recently emancipated saw their rights taken away once more. Within a few short years, black political power was all but snuffed out. By the start of the 20th century, Louisiana, home of the New Orleans Mint, had fewer than 6,000 blacks registered to vote, despite the fact that the state was predominantly black.

Poor whites, too, suffered under the yoke of oppression. Across the country, laborers struggled to survive. In the Midwest, poor farmers barely grew enough crops to feed their families. Mortgages on family farms had most farmers in debt, even though the lands an increasing number of Midwesterners had settled on had been purchased by the federal government from displaced Native Americans for pennies on the dollar.

Titans of industry loomed large over the American experience. Men like Andrew Carnegie, John Pierpont Morgan, and John D. Rockefeller muscled, coerced, and sometimes brutal-

In the Wild West of the late 1800s, bandits like Black Bart still prowled the back roads and byways. Their hauls may have included some Morgan dollars.

ANOTHER OF OUR EXPORTS;—THE AMERICAN FORTUNE.

America in the age of the Morgan dollar was a land of great wealth, but also had its share of poverty and struggle.

4

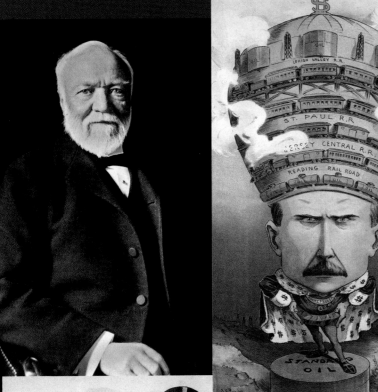

Captains of industry like Andrew Carnegie, J.P. Morgan, and John D. Rockefeller were constantly in the news during the Morgan dollar era.

ized workers in order to build enormous empires of wealth. Through their power and influence, the country's elites used government as an instrument to get what they wanted.

For the wealthy and the privileged, the "Gilded Age" had arrived.

The prosperity of the Gilded Age wouldn't have been possible without improvements in manufacturing. Massive industries were created, and Americans began to shift away from their agrarian roots for factory jobs in the major cities. For wealthy industrialists, this period marked the beginning of the welfare state as the government doled out corporate welfare to the well-connected, giving free land to railroad companies, free money to big banks, and proposing a panoply of favorable legislation to those whose connections and purse strings could persuade their elected representatives.

Across the country, factories began to pop up with increased frequency. America's industrial sector was revolutionized by the ability to move goods across the country quickly and cheaply due to the rapid expansion of the nation's railroad infrastructure. Great sums of money were being made by the captains of American industry while the working class toiled under difficult and sometimes dangerous work conditions, working long hours for little pay.

The Americans of this period soldiered on. Many organized to demand better pay and better working conditions. The American labor movement entered the scene.

At the beginning of the Morgan dollar's run, the most recent state to join the Union was mineral-rich Colorado. In 1878, Colorado was teeming with activity as miners descended upon the new state in search of silver and gold. Colorado was also a tinderbox of racial tension between white settlers and Chinese immigrants who had come to the area willing to work cheap.

The Chinese weren't the only people who left everything behind for a chance at a new life. For many, the close of the 19th century was a period of growth and new opportunities. The American West called to tens of thousands of settlers who cobbled together their possessions and gathered their families for the promise of a better future. At the crossroads of that future were the many native tribes for whom this great migration of settlers proved an existential threat.

THE GREAT WEST

The Great American West beckoned as a land of opportunity in the 1800s.

Gaylord Watson
No. 61 BEEKMAN ST.
NEW YORK.

PUBLISHED
BY
AND

Tenney & Weaver
No. 6 WASHINGTON ST.
CHICAGO, ILLS.

The Morgan dollar circulated at a time when the great Chief Sitting Bull still roamed the Dakota wilderness. The Morgan dollar flowed through the freewheeling Bird Cage saloon of the silver-mining town of Tombstone, Arizona, where, in October 1881, a gunfight broke out at the O.K. Corral. The first skyscraper, a ten-story-high brick-and-mortar edifice, was completed in Chicago, solidifying the career of Louis Sullivan and launching a whole school of American architects. After several labor riots ended in tragedy, the eight-hour workday was legislated. Coca-Cola debuted. Susan B. Anthony, the subject of a much later dollar coin, agitated for women's rights. Schoolchildren across the country first recited the Pledge of Allegiance. Coxey's

Writer Mark Twain entertained America with his unique voice and characters.

Social leaders like Elizabeth Cady Stanton and Susan B. Anthony fought for equal rights for women.

Booker T. Washington—educator, author, orator, and presidential advisor—was a force for civil rights.

Army marched on Washington to rally against unemployment and protest economic policies.

Booker T. Washington and W.E.B. Du Bois blazed different trails to better the lives of American blacks while the U.S. Supreme Court propped up the doctrine of "separate but equal." American writer Mark Twain captivated generations of American readers with his sardonic wit and quintessentially American novels.

The United States entered into a war against Spain that saw U.S. troops in the Caribbean and as far away as the Philippine Islands. Major-league baseball grew into the national pastime. A hurricane in Galveston, Texas, would be the worst natural disaster in U.S. history, rivaled only by Katrina. In the same state, oil was discovered in great abundance.

The America that circulated the Morgan dollar was full of marvels, alive with wonder and opportunity, innovation, and scientific breakthroughs the likes of which the world had never seen. While George T. Morgan's Miss Liberty made the rounds, the Wizard of Menlo Park—Thomas Alva Edison—was developing commercial applications for electricity. Standard Oil, the predecessor of Exxon Mo-

Thomas Alva Edison in 1878, the year he patented the phonograph—and the year the Morgan dollar debuted.

bil, was founded. The Brooklyn Bridge opened to the public. The world's first rodeo was held. The Statue of Liberty, a gift from the people of France, was assembled in New York, while a few hundred miles south, the Washington Monument, 40 years in the making, was completed. Orville Wright flew the first airplane at Kitty Hawk, North Carolina.

The United States endured two depressions during this time: one lasting four years from 1882 to 1885 and another from 1893 to 1897. The federal government began the regulation of corporations and big business. Full of optimism about America and American society, the Progressive Era hit full stride, and at the end of its run the first Miss America Pageant was held in Atlantic City, New Jersey.

The Morgan dollar spanned from the Reconstruction to just past the end of World War I. By then, it was an old-fashioned reminder of an important period of American history, the romantic ideal of a great nation in ascendance.

George T. Morgan's iconic dollar design was replaced by a coin agitated for by the American Numismatic Association. That coin was called the Peace dollar, in honor of the end of what everyone hoped would be the "war to end all wars." Once again, America steeled its resolve and took its place on the world stage as a beacon of hope, the shining light on the hill.

Problems with Money

It's hard to imagine today, but during the Civil War, Americans lived in a volatile economic environment with different currencies circulating side by side. Goods could be bought with Postage Currency, greenbacks, Confederate currency, bronze tokens, copper and nickel coinage, silver coinage and bullion, and gold coinage and bullion. The preferred medium of exchange of all these was gold. A gold dollar had one dollar of purchasing power. Silver was accepted at a reduced rate. Paper currency, if accepted at all, bought even less.

Legal Tender Notes were the first issue of modern federal paper currency—an invention of the early 1860s, used to finance the Union's massive Civil War efforts.

Much of this was theoretical, as Americans during the war hoarded their coins—not just gold and silver, but even humble copper-and–nickel cents.

This discrepancy wrought confusion in the economy, and along with that confusion came double-digit inflation. By war's end, the government sought to return to a specie standard and began to redeem outstanding currency notes. The debate over what the specie standard should look like played out on the national stage and repeatedly within the halls of Congress. Two major factions were born: the Silverites and the Gold Bugs.

The Silverites advocated for a return to the bimetallic standard laid out in the Coinage Act of 1792. That act called for the ratio of silver's value to gold to be set at 15:1, meaning fifteen ounces of silver had the same *legal* purchasing power as one ounce of gold. Almost immediately, and due in large part to the French Revolution, the value of gold had increased relative to silver. This pushed gold out of circulation until reforms to American coinage law took effect in 1834.

The legislation of 1834 changed the bimetallic ratio to 16:1. This shift in price had as much to do with

Silverites and Gold Bugs duked it out in editorial cartoons, newspaper columns, and public discussions of the late 1800s. These covers from the New York City–based humor magazine *Puck* portray Silverites as hayseed rubes, obstructionists, and villains.

Rutherford Hayes was the governor of Ohio before being elected president in 1876. The first Morgan dollars rolled off the presses during his administration.

the world market as it had to do with President Andrew Jackson's desire to smash the Bank of the United States. The Bank, according to Jackson and his supporters, had grown too powerful. Jackson's 16:1 gold supporters (rural, small-business, lower-class Southerners and Westerners) were the same constituency that would support William Jennings Bryan in his anti-gold platform of 1896. The mutual foes of both groups were essentially the same: powerful, well-connected Northerners, big banks, and big business.

The Gold Bugs sought to keep gold decoupled from silver, citing the facts that the market value of silver no longer equaled 16:1 and that the United States government did not have the means, legislative or otherwise, to make it so.

The argument between the two factions developed in the aftermath of the Coinage Act of 1873, which silver proponents dubbed the "Crime of 1873." The act demonetized silver, authorized the production of a silver bullion coin called the trade dollar, and effectively set the United States on the gold standard. It passed with little controversy.

In 1876, Republican Rutherford B. Hayes became president thanks to a deal reached with Southern Democrats whereby Reconstruction was brought to an end and the last federal troops were withdrawn from the South.

Hayes was firmly against bimetallism. So, in 1878, when Representative Richard P. Bland (D-Missouri) and Senator William B. Allison (R-Iowa) worked out a version of the Bland-Allison Act that could pass both houses of Congress, Hayes threatened to veto it. The act provided for the coinage of up to four million silver dollars every month, and was close to what the Silverites (and Western mining interests) wanted.

The bill passed and, true to his word, President Hayes vetoed it. Congress then overrode his veto. Thus the Morgan dollar was born.

This $50 Silver Certificate, from the Series of 1878, was payable in the form of 50 silver dollar coins from the vaults of the New York Sub-Treasury.

The next major piece of legislation concerning the controversy was the Sherman Silver Purchase Act of 1890. It required the government to buy 4.5 million ounces of silver bullion a month, replacing the Bland-Allison Act. The Silver Purchase Act also required that the silver be bought with special Treasury Notes that could be redeemed in either silver or gold. Predictably, people chose to redeem their notes in the more valuable gold, which exacerbated an already metastasizing financial crisis that lead to the Panic and Depression of 1893. President Grover Cleveland oversaw the act's repeal shortly thereafter.

1896 saw famed congressman and orator Williams Jennings Bryan accept the Democratic nomination for the presidency. Bryan was perhaps the most well-known supporter of bimetallism and Free Silver, delivering the famous "Cross of Gold" speech at that year's Democratic National Convention. The Republicans nominated William McKinley, who supported a policy of "sound money," effectively meaning that the United States should be on the gold standard.

Bryan lost to McKinley and fought a rematch in 1900. He lost again, but the free coining of silver and bimetallism was already a lost cause—the Gold Standard Act of 1900 firmly entrenched gold as the basis for America's money until the Great Depression.

The Peculiar Fate of the Morgan Dollar

Whether the Morgan dollar existed merely to make a political point is debatable. The fact remains that it spent much of its first century locked away in Treasury vaults. This, however, creates something of a false impression, because for many Americans the coin served its purpose. The large dollar coin circulated in pockets of the Western interior—states such as Montana, Utah, and Nevada. The coin also circulated in California, where the abundance of gold made the standard of living higher there than elsewhere in the country. In the East, the Morgan dollar entered into the streams of commerce as well, though not at a pace that justified its hitherto unheard-of mintages.

The total duration of the coin's production life spanned 43 years. The Morgan dollar was struck continuously for 26 years before a 17-year-long hiatus left the Mint without workable hubs, after which the coin made its unexpected return in 1921. Its ready availability at face value lasted through early 1964, a period of 85 years. As of now, only the Lincoln cent has lasted longer (though the Washington quarter and Jefferson nickel aren't far behind).

Excepting Liberty Head double eagles, the Morgan dollar is the only 19th-century coin readily found today in Mint State. When it was made, it was the most voluminously produced coin in U.S. history, with a final tally exceeding 500 million coins. Great melts, including the one compelled by the Pittman Act in 1918, wiped out more than 270 million of those coins—a total that would be enough to eradicate nearly every coin ever struck for any other 19th-century series. For the Morgan dollar, the melt only added to the intrigue, as collectors never really knew which issues were destroyed or how many of each issue remained.

The Peace Silver dollar would eventually replace George Morgan's design, in 1921.

This uncertainty shaped the early years of the growing Morgan dollar market. Coins once considered rare sprang up in tremendous quantities just when numismatics was taking hold as a mainstream—and profitable—pursuit. Other issues, long thought common due to the reported number of coins struck, were revealed to be scarce as demand increased and few new pieces entered the market.

Today, the Morgan dollar is the most robust collectible of its era in American numismatics and traded in a highly sophisticated market, with untold thousands of collectors building collections as individual as the collectors themselves.

It is also the most collected 19th-century United States coin in the history of American numismatics. This wasn't always the case: the Morgan dollar, for all its unique charm and historical significance, was long neglected by those who saw its ready availability as a detriment to its worth as a collectible coin.

In the following chapters, you will see how all this changed.

Chapter Two

Anatomy of a Dollar: A Brief Look at Design

Obverse

The Morgan dollar is one of the most distinctive coins ever produced by the United States, and at the time of its initial release it was the most sophisticated coin design yet executed by the U.S. Mint.

The coin's designer, George T. Morgan, was hired for the express purpose of elevating the artistic quality of American coinage, which, according to Mint Director Henry Linderman, had "not been brought to much perfection." The idea that Linderman had to bring in outside talent to do this did not sit well with Chief Engraver William Barber and his son Charles. They made their displeasure clear by creating a hostile atmosphere for the new engraver. This forced Morgan to work outside of the Mint building when developing the artistic elements that would go into the new coin. But in light of Linderman's own assessment of the Mint, Morgan's ostracism couldn't have been more fortuitous.

A fresh yet respectful approach was brought to bear. Morgan carried forward traditional American thematic elements, such as the Phrygian cap, the Liberty crown, and the heraldic eagle and stars, and coupled them with a European sensibility born from the Beaux Arts School of classical design. The result was a pastiche of both old and new.

In other words, the coin was quintessentially American.

Liberty

It's long been believed that the model for the Morgan dollar was a 19-year-old Philadelphia woman named Anna Willess Williams. The story goes that in 1876, while Morgan was hard at work preparing models for new coin designs, he was introduced to Williams by his friend Thomas Eakins, a widely renowned painter active in the Philadelphia art scene. Williams was said to have reluctantly posed for Morgan in November of that year, sitting five times before the master engraver.

The sittings were supposed to remain a secret. However, word spread in 1879 that Williams was the model, based on a report written by a pesky newspaperman who happened to notice a similarity between Williams and the portrait on the dollar. Offers of celebrity poured in to Williams, who spurned them all for a quiet life of educating children.

When Williams died of complications from a hip injury in 1926, she was 68 years old. The "Silver Dollar Girl" survived the coin by five years. A story recounting the details of her life and death, and her presumed role in American numismatic history, ran that year in the April 26 issue of *Time* magazine.

In recent years, the identity of the model for the coin has come into question. Paul Gilkes, a writer for *Coin World,* published a piece in 2002 that described an undated letter from the daughter of George T. Morgan written to her granddaughter, wherein the former chief engraver had allegedly refuted the notion that any real model served as the basis of the dollar coin. Does this private letter between family members undo a century of scholarship? One has to wonder.

At any rate, when we look at Morgan's artistic interpretation of Liberty, we see the bold figure of a Greek goddess. Her hair flows down in an intricate manner, loose locks jutting out with naturalistic irregularity. Morgan pulls her hair back just enough to reveal the bottom of her earlobe.

Liberty's chin is rounded and pronounced, as are her pouting lips. A slight slope distinguishes her profile from the tip of her nose to the top of her forehead. A sharp angle at the hollow of her throat marks the tip of the bust's truncation. Another slight curve marks the bottom of the figure. Morgan's initial, M, is inscribed here, in intaglio, as part of the line.

George Morgan's initial, M.

Curiously, Liberty is depicted without pupils. In Greek statuary, pupils were painted over the relief. This design detail was a first for an American coin.

Miss Liberty's eye;
note the lack of pupil.

Cap

Liberty wears a cone-shaped cloth headpiece called a Phrygian cap. The Phrygian cap traces its origins back to antiquity. In Roman times it was associated with freedmen, or former slaves. The cap, along with the liberty pole (another Roman symbol), played a role in rallying the colonies against British rule during the build-up to the Revolutionary War.

The cap-and-pole motif adorned several post-colonial copper issues before appearing on federal coinage for the first time in 1793 on the half cent and the large cent.

The liberty cap and pole on a half cent of 1793.

The series that Morgan replaced, Christian Gobrecht's Liberty Seated dollar, also features the cap-and-pole motif. In that instance, Liberty is holding the liberty pole in her left hand while the cap sits on top.

The liberty cap and pole as featured on Christian Gobrecht's Liberty Seated dollar.

Morgan's Liberty dons the cap, which is depicted as delicate and billowy. A thin ribbon wraps around the base and is hard to see without close inspection.

Another detail that might escape the casual observer is that Liberty is wearing something called a "vegetal" wreath. Vegetal wreaths have a long tradition in numismatics, and, like the Phrygian cap, are an ancient motif.

A ribbon wraps at the base of Miss Liberty's Phrygian cap.

In the United States, wreaths appeared on federal coins almost from the outset, with the aptly named 1793 Wreath cent. In 1856 Chief Engraver James B. Longacre introduced a new kind of wreath to American coinage. The reverse of his Flying Eagle cent features a vegetal wreath made of corn, tobacco, cotton, and wheat.

Morgan continues this theme, but reduces it to two symbolic crops: wheat and cotton. By using the most prominent crops of the North and South, the Morgan dollar makes a strong yet subliminal statement about the indivisibility of our great nation and the equality of its component parts.

A vegetal wreath.

Stars

Thirteen stars—representing the thirteen original states of the Union—wrap around the coin's southern hemisphere. The entire array is slightly canted to the left and broken up by the sharp angular wedge of Liberty's neck. The stars are six-pointed, similar to but smaller than the ones found on the reverse. Each star on the obverse is oriented so that a ray points to the coin's rim.

Each obverse star points to the dollar's rim.

Mottos and Legends

The obverse features the motto E PLURIBUS UNUM, and the legend LIBERTY.

E Pluribus Unum, a Latin phrase that can be taken to mean either "Out of Many (States), One (Nation)" or "Out of Many (People), One (Nation)", first appeared on post-colonial American issues in 1786, adorning the reverse of the New Jersey copper. Use of the motto spread to other states shortly thereafter. It appeared on the 1787 Excelsior copper (New York), the 1787 Brasher doubloon (also from New York), and later the Kentucky token series.

The inscription E PLURIBUS UNUM was adopted as part of the Great Seal of the United States in 1782. The seal was incorporated into Mint engraver Robert Scot's Capped Bust gold half-eagle design in 1795, which is how E PLURIBUS UNUM made its federal coin debut.

LIBERTY is inscribed in Miss Liberty's crown. Underappreciated Mint engraver John Reich introduced the symbolic motif to United States coins in 1807, with the Capped Bust half eagle and half dollar. The motif caught on and quickly found its way onto other denominations, starting with the large cent and quarter eagle in 1808, the half cent and dime in 1809, the quarter in 1815, and so on. . . .

Interestingly enough, the Morgan dollar was the first silver dollar to use a "Liberty crown," as production of the denomination was suspended at the time Reich introduced the motif. When the silver dollar coin was resurrected in 1836, it bore Christian Gobrecht's Liberty Seated design. The Mint's chief engraver instead opted to drape the legend across a federal shield that Miss Liberty appears to be holding. The Liberty Seated dollar went into wide-scale production in 1840 and continued to serve as America's dollar coin until Congress discontinued its production in 1873.

LIBERTY is marked on Miss Liberty's headgear.

Dates

The date is presented below the truncation of the bust, nestled in between seven stars on the left and six on the right. The position of the date on the coin was static for the first six years of production, with the last digits being edited for each subsequent year. Morgan dollar variety experts have noted numerous date positions thereafter, many of which are highly collectible varieties.

Denticles

Denticles, also called dentils, are the small, *tooth*-like moldings around the perimeter of a coin—hence the name. Denticles form the highest point on a coin and are designed to protect it from excessive wear. They also help stack one coin on top of another. This design feature went out of style with the introduction of the steam press.

You may not have noticed, but there's a 2 percent difference in the size of the denticles on the obverse and reverse of the Morgan dollar. The obverse has 148 denticles, while the reverse has 151. In Van Allen and Mallis's *Encyclopedia of Morgan & Peace Dollars,* the authors point to the work of variety expert Pete Bishal, who studied the issue and noted that on early patterns the number of denticles on each side was actually reversed! Why Morgan made the change, no one knows. But it's a great piece of trivia.

Tooth-like denticles surround the fields of the Morgan dollar.

Rims

On circulation strikes, the coin's denticles blend into the rims. On Proof strikes, the rims have a squared appearance and there's a clear separation between the two design elements.

Reeding

Morgan dollars have reeded edges. Reeds are vertical ridges on the side of a coin, imparted by a collar die and originally used to discourage the clipping of coins to shave off silver and gold.

The number of reeds on a Morgan dollar varies by year and mint. Typically, a Morgan dollar will have 189 reeds, but this number can go as high as 194 and as low as 157. Also, in recent years some examples have been discovered with overlapping reeding (e.g., the 1900-O VAM 50).

Reeding on the edge of the Morgan dollar.

Reverse

Eagle

Whereas Morgan drew from neoclassical tradition for his Grecian effigy on the obverse, he presents us with a detailed ornithological rendering of an eagle on the reverse. It is a vast improvement over Gobrecht's sitting eagle from the Liberty Seated design and William Barber's rather contorted and strange-looking trade-dollar eagle.

As is customary, Morgan depicted the eagle with an olive branch in its right, or *dexter,* talon and three arrows in its left, or *sinister,* talon. The eagle's head is turned toward the right, presumably as a symbol that the United States prefers peace to war.

Critics of the day were unimpressed. In his *Encyclopedia,* Bowers mentions a *Harper's Weekly* piece on the coin that said the eagle "doesn't seem to resemble a bird of our country. In fact, we are afraid the thing is a British grouse." The grousing (pun intended) was unwarranted, because a grouse doesn't have an eagle's hooked beak—a detail obviously rendered in Morgan's design.

Later, Morgan reprised his eagle design for the reverse of the 1915 Panama-Pacific Exposition commemorative half dollar. There, it's perched atop a federal shield. A wreath of oak and olive branches springs forth, surrounding the eagle in a fashion similar to Morgan's dollar design.

George Morgan's design for the reverse of the 1915 Panama-Pacific Exposition half dollar uses an eagle reminiscent of his famous dollar.

Wreath

Morgan employs an open wreath design for the reverse, made of berries and olive leaves. The olive branch is a well-known symbol of peace. Five sprigs fan out on each side. Each sprig has five to seven leaves, but the left and right sides of the wreath are asymmetrical. Sixteen berries populate the wreath on most issues. In the 1921, new hubs for the Morgan dollar were created, and certain Philly strikes feature a reverse with 17 berries.

The initial of Morgan's last name can be found in the ribbon of the bow.

Morgan's initial, M, appears on the ribbon that ties the wreath on the reverse.

Mottos and Legends

Wrapping around the top 80 percent of the coin's perimeter is the legend UNITED STATES OF AMERICA. The eagle's outstretched wings divide UNITED from STATES and OF from AMERICA. A similar composition was used on the dollars of 1798 to 1804.

The motto IN GOD WE TRUST appears over the eagle's head. While the motto also appeared in this location on the trade dollar and the silver dollar of 1866 to 1873, it's worth mentioning that the area above the eagle's head was used for religious symbolism well before the motto's introduction in 1864. It was the common location of a heraldic motif known as a Circle of Glory, or simply the Glory. The Glory is a ring of light surrounded by clouds that demonstrates the presence of God.

On American coinage, this is represented by clouds and 13 stars, each star standing for one of the original 13 states. Glories can be seen on Draped Bust silver coins and Heraldic Eagle–reverse Capped Bust gold, Liberty Head double eagles, and some commemorative designs. Even the American Silver Eagle bullion coin references the motif on its reverse.

The motto IN GOD WE TRUST is in blackletter or Old English script.

Denomination

Believe it or not, many of America's earliest silver and gold coins did not include a readily obvious inscription stating the coin's value. While the half cent and large cent both debuted in 1793 with their stated values on the reverse, the half dime and half dollar, both silver coins, did not. (Their denominations were lettered on their edges.) In 1795 the half eagle and eagle—both gold coins—similarly debuted *sans* denominational identification on front or back, and the dime, quarter dollar, and quarter eagle followed suit a year later.

An early U.S. silver half dollar and $10 gold coin— their reverses bore no indication of their denomination.

A lack of immediate clarity in terms of value did little to help the pieces circulate as money. With the predominance of foreign coins and the lack of sufficient production capacity (not to mention an untenable bimetallic ratio of 15 to 1), it's little surprise that these early coins were traded based on their bullion value.

The Mint sought to remedy this problem with the first major design changes starting in 1807, when the new half dollar included the inscription 50 C. on the reverse. Other silver and gold denominations followed suit, and by 1815 almost all U.S. coins in production had a statement of value as part of their reverse design.

But two denominations were noticeably absent: the silver dollar and the gold eagle. Both denominations saw heavy exportation and led President Thomas Jefferson to cease production of the coins and focus on making smaller-denomination gold and silver instead, which he hoped would circulate in the new country.

It wasn't until the Mint tried to reintroduce the silver dollar in 1836 that the denomination first bore the obvious inscription ONE DOLLAR. When the coin finally went into widespread circulation in 1840, the inscription changed to ONE DOL. Morgan's design returned ONE DOLLAR to the reverse, placing it at the bottom and wrapping it around the coin's outer perimeter.

Before the 1830s, U.S. silver dollars carried their denomination on their edge. Starting with the Gobrecht dollar the denomination would be on the coin's reverse.

Mintmark

The use of mintmarks in the United States started after the Act of March 3, 1835, which authorized the opening of branch mints in Charlotte (North Carolina), Dahlonega (Georgia), and New Orleans (Louisiana).

A mintmark is a symbol on a coin, in addition to the normal design elements, that identifies the facility responsible for producing it. By adopting this age-old practice, the Mint was able to retain central control over coin production as coins that failed to meet legal standards could be traced back to their source.

Mintmarks of four of the mints that struck Morgan dollars—Carson City, Denver, New Orleans, and San Francisco. (Coins of the fifth, the main mint in Philadelphia, featured no mintmark.)

Coins struck at the main mint in Philadelphia bear no mintmark. Coins struck at the branch mints included a letter (or in the case of Carson City, two letters) signifying their mint of origin.

The mintmarks used on Morgan dollars are as follows: CC for Carson City, Nevada (1878–1885, 1889–1893), D for Denver, Colorado (1921), O for New Orleans, Louisiana (1879–1904), and S for San Francisco, California (1878–1921).

Mintmarks on the Morgan dollar are located in the space above the letters DO in DOLLAR on the reverse, below the bow at the center of the wreath. Numerous varieties involving mintmarks are known to exist.

Stars

The stars on the coin's reverse are slightly larger than the stars on the obverse. The simple fact that there are only two of them gave Morgan more space to fill around the coin's perimeter. The stars, like those on the obverse, are positioned so that one ray points straight to the denticles. If you draw an imaginary line from this tip through the star and toward the center of the coin, you will find that both lines intersect in the center.

Chapter Three

The Morgan Dollar Series: A Market Study Revisited

The 26th edition of the *Red Book*, dated 1973, featured a seminal study on the development of the Morgan dollar market. Taking prices from the first edition of the *Red Book* (1947) and charting the growth of the market over the subsequent 25 years, the editors of the book examined the changes in collector attitude toward the series and showed how prices fluctuated over the course of a quarter century.

The analysis was especially timely. The General Services Administration had just launched the highest-profile mail-bid auction in the history of numismatics: the historic GSA sale of nearly three million mostly Uncirculated Carson City Morgan dollars.

Among the various tidbits offered by the editors were two key facts that set the Morgan dollar apart from other popularly collected series. One was that the mammoth amount of untouched, collectible-quality dollar coins gave collectors an "unprecedented 'second chance.'" The other was that there was "no certainty about the quantity available of any date or mint mark."

Certainly, both points were true when the editors were preparing the 26th edition. And while the lack of real information regarding availability had a stifling effect on the market when the government was sitting on millions of unsearched and uncirculated Morgan dollars, once those coins were released, the dearth of publicized caches of particular issues amplified collector interest in those issues almost immediately.

The truth is, *Red Book* editor Richard S. Yeoman and virtually every clued-in coin dealer or collector had a much firmer grasp on the Morgan dollar market in 1973 than he and his top-tier contributors (Aubrey Bebee, Abe Kosoff, Abner Kreisberg, Stuart Mosher, and Farran Zerbe to name but a few) had in 1946, when the 1947 edition was prepared. In the first edition, they stated that the non-existent 1895 circulation strike was worth $6.00, the same figure they gave for the 1878 Eight Tail Feathers.

Still, even with the distribution of the government's holdings, and despite the arrival in the early 1960s of the *Coin Dealer Newsletter* and of electronic Teletype-based trading platforms, a clear picture of the available quantities for each issue didn't fully develop for another 10 to 20 years.

The potential for privately held hoards was apparent. Some collectors and dealers have always squirreled away coins in anticipation of a strong future market and greater returns. Even speculators without numismatic training were getting in on the action, thanks to books like George W. Haylings's popular *The Profit March of Your Coin Investment* (1971), which didn't deal with dollar coins specifically but did claim that common-date small-denomination coinage would one day reap future profits.

This optimism, coupled with the withdrawal of silver from circulation, delayed a final verdict on which Morgan dollar issues were rare and which ones weren't. This didn't stop the market, however. In fact, it did just the opposite—it made expansion of the Morgan dollar market possible. The uncertainty effectively prolonged collector interest in the series and put the Morgan dollar in the spotlight as the most collectible series of 19th-century United States coins—a mantle the Morgan dollar has yet to relinquish, and probably never will.

Those Large Silver Cartwheels

That the Morgan dollar hit its stride as a collectible and investment coin *after* the removal of silver from our nation's circulating coinage is no surprise.

Silver had been a part of the United States' monetary system since even before Congress authorized the creation of the U.S. Mint in 1792. The first coin ever struck by the federal government was a silver half disme (likely pronounced "deem"), a small five-cent coin that, as tradition has it, was made with silver from Martha Washington's table service. Silver had served an important if often subsidiary role in our economy for more than 173 years before Congress, at the urging of President Lyndon Johnson, enacted legislation that replaced the precious metal with a cheaper alloy made of copper and nickel.

The change sent shockwaves through numismatic circles. Collectors feared that an end to silver-coin production would hurt the hobby. The Treasury Department worried about hoarding, and for a brief time suspended the use of mintmarks and enacted a date freeze. The impact of the changeover is still felt today, as many numismatists see it as the dividing line between what's collectible and what's not.

From an economic standpoint, many Americans were concerned that the change in alloy would cause inflation. Some even grew concerned that the new coins wouldn't be accepted as legal tender (they weren't always accepted at overseas military installations). Despite the government's prohibition of the melting and export of silver coinage, and the president's assurances that clad and silver coins would long serve side by side, the public's extraction of all pre-1965 silver coinage began almost immediately.

The Johnson administration had prepared for this contingency by ordering the concurrent production of silver dimes, quarters, and half dollars (all bearing the date 1964) until enough copper-nickel-clad dimes, quarters, and half dollars in the new tenor (all dated 1965 or later) could be struck to satisfy the needs of the economy. The last of the 90 percent silver coins rolled off the presses in 1964.

The extraction of silver coins from circulation by hoarders, speculators, and romantics is the result of an economic principle called Gresham's Law, which says that bad money chases good money out of circulation.

Just as cheaper silver coinage made people think twice about using gold as money in the

19th century, cheap clad coins pushed silver out of circulation in the 20th. Two metals of different intrinsic values never circulate side by side as equals. Not for long, anyway.

The extraction of silver coinage from circulation was swift, which contributed to an influx of new collectors into the market. Many who had used silver their whole lives, only to see it disappear, suddenly wanted one more chance to hold onto it.

Speculators also saw bigger yields buying large volumes of numismatic material over junk silver, as the growing coin market promised handsome returns for those who had collectible coins to sell.

For both types of buyer, one coin stood out above all others: the large "cartwheel" silver dollar. Not only was the silver dollar the largest of the silver coins, it was also seen as the most collectible due to the high-profile nature of the Treasury releases of the 1960s. When the Treasury Department stopped offering the coins at face value, they gained immediate numismatic value.

How much of this value was based originally on demand versus marketing is debatable. What is indisputable, however, is that it didn't take long for the dollar market to take off, led by the beautiful Morgan. The dollar coin the 19th century didn't want quickly became the most popular collector's coin in the marketplace.

A Tale of Two Markets: Winners and Losers

First-Edition *Red Book*

The first edition of the *Red Book* gives two pages of coverage to the Morgan dollar. The minimalist presentation mentions no varieties, save the 8 and 7 Tail Feathers varieties of 1878. Mintage information is included not in the coin-by-coin pages but in a separate appendix in the back (the "Quantity Minted" column would debut in the 16th edition).

Unlike today's eight-column *Red Book* pricing grid, which features stepped valuations in circulated and Uncirculated grades, the 1947 edition provides only two pricing columns: "Uncirculated" and "Proof." In total, postwar collectors are presented a series with 23 price points.

These price points can be broken down into four tiers:

Common ($2.00 to $2.75) . . . . 23 coins

Semi-common ($3.00 to $6.00) . . . 31 coins

Scarce ($7.50 to $15.00) . . . . 36 coins

Rare ($45.00 and up) . . . . 3 coins

As you'd expect, the prices given are *retail* price points. The common-tier coins would have brought little premium over face

value if someone were to sell them to a dealer. That's because Morgan dollars were readily available by the bag from most banks. For the most common issues, the retail price is simply a convenience fee for getting the coin you want without the hassle of going to a bank.

Common-Tier Morgan Dollars (1947 *Red Book*)—$2.00 to $2.75		
$2.00	**$2.50**	**$2.75**
1921	1878-S	1879
	1879-S	1886-S
	1880	1898-S
	1881	
	1880-S	
	1881-S	
	1882	
	1882-S	
	1883	
	1884	
	1887-S	
	1888-S	
	1889-S	
	1890-S	
	1891-S	
	1900-S	
	1904	
	1921-D	
	1921-S	

Of all the Morgan dollars struck, the 1921 is by far the most common. In 1947 the coin had the least collector value of any coin in the series. In fact, many dealers who advertised a desire to purchase Morgan dollars flatly declared that they did not want any dollars from 1921. This sentiment remained in effect for decades and only started to lift when the market matured to the point where premium money was being paid for high-end coins.

The second band of the common tier includes 19 coins at the $2.50 price point. Adjusted for inflation, a Morgan dollar worth $2.50 then amounts to $26.18 in 2014 money, with approximately $8 of that $26 being the inflation-adjusted 1947 price of silver. Depending on the spot price of bullion, this figure isn't far removed from the current generic wholesale price of circulated Morgans today.

Experienced Morgan dollar collectors will look at the list above and notice several issues that were seriously undervalued at the time. All of the San Francisco issues on the list (starting with 1887 and running through 1900) are considered better dates now, with Gems (MS-65 and better) of any of these easily bringing more than a thousand dollars in today's market. The biggest winner of the bunch is the 1888-S, which currently goes for more than $400 in MS-63 and $2,500 in MS-65.

For a quarter more, the 1947 *Red Book* suggests that you can buy the 1879 Philly-strike or the 1886-S and 1898-S. Of these three issues, the San Francisco releases turned out to be the clear winners. The 1879 remains a common-date Morgan dollar, but the 1886-S and 1898-S are scarce in Mint State.

The 1886-S had a mintage of under a million, and collectors have the Redfield Hoard to thank for infusing the market with approximately 3,000 pieces in the 1970s. The 1898-S has a mintage over four times greater, but is frustratingly less available in Mint State. To make matters worse, most are poorly struck, not a usual feature of San Francisco Morgans.

If nothing I've written so far demonstrates how unsettled the Morgan dollar series was as a collectible, the table above should settle the matter. With real bargains to be found in every column, plus an impossible coin (I'll get to that later), a collector in 1947 who stocked up on coins listed at $3.00 to $6.00 would have made out really well given today's prices.

In the $3.00 column, the 1885 and 1888 remained common, but the 1892 and 1899-S did not. Today, those two fetch $400 to $500 in MS-63.

The coin with the biggest upside in the table is the 1901, which was listed for $3.25. A dealer in 1947 might have paid half that for a brilliant Uncirculated example. Now, you can't even sniff this coin in MS-63 for under $15,000.

The $3.50 column is a mixed bag. The 1891 and 1897-S command two to three times the price of a common-date Morgan. The lone Carson City dollar, the 1884-CC was mostly distributed through the GSA hoard in the 1970s. These days, it's a $250 coin in a GSA holder (more if it's a nice example). The 1893, with just 378,000 minted at the outset of a major economic crisis, is the easiest of the date's four Morgan dollar issues, but it's still a thousand-dollar coin today in MS-63. The 1894, the lowest-produced Philadelphia Morgan circulation strike, is almost unheard of in Uncirculated condition; you'd assume it was equally unheard of in the 1940s as well. Modern demand for the coin is so great that even well-worn examples command a thousand dollars or more. In Mint State, the coin sells for $5,000 in MS-63 and over $40,000 for a Gem.

In the $3.75 and $4.00 columns, the two Carson City issues—1890-CC and 1891-CC—are better dates. The 1899 and 1902 command a modest premium. The 1904-S, one of the poorest-quality San Francisco issues of the series, might not have been much to get excited about at the time, but today it's seldom seen in Mint State. A choice example of this penultimate release will set you back about $4,000.

There are clear winners from $5.00 to $6.00, and clear losers. There's also an impossible listing. For starters, the 1878, 8 Tail Feathers, is obviously an important coin since it was the first Morgan dollar design released for circulation. Its current market value illustrates strong demand for this important type coin. The 1882-CC and 1883-CC appear to benefit from their connection to Carson City and the Old West, because both of these are readily available due to the GSA hoard. But like the 1878, 8 Tail Feathers, today they command $200 and up in MS-63.

Semi-Common-Tier Morgan Dollars (1947 *Red Book*)—$3.00 to $6.00							
$3.00	$3.25	$3.50	$3.75	$4.00	$5.00	$5.50	$6.00
1885	1901	1883-O	1891-CC	1886	1878 8TF	1878-CC	1878 7TF
1888		1884-O		1890-CC	1882-CC	1883-S	1895
1892		1884-CC		1898	1883-CC		1896
1899-S		1887		1899	1885-O		
		1889		1902	1890-O		
		1890		1904-S	1897		
		1891			1903		
		1893					
		1894					
		1897-S					
		1900					

The 1878-CC, listed in the $5.50 column, fares better than the other Carson City issues, in large part because only 47,000 were included in the GSA sale.

The 1883-S was the diamond in the rough. San Francisco's production of dollar coins kept pace with Philadelphia in the first years of the series. By 1883, it became clear that the West Coast mint would soon run out of storage capacity, as there was little demand for the coin at the time. This led to a 33 percent reduction in the number of dollars struck, which one assumes should still have been enough to leave today's collector with plenty of inventory. Not so—the 1883-S is surprisingly elusive, with most examples probably having met their end in the smelter's pot. A choice example will set you back $2,500.

Which brings us to the 1895. Crypto-numismatists—collectors who search for rumored coins, presumed to exist but never seen—were so committed to the mistaken belief that circulation-strike 1895s had been struck that the "issue" ranked 39th in terms of price in the 1947 *Red Book*. In all likelihood, most of the 1895 dollars passed off as circulation strikes were actually Proofs, which would still have made the coin a good buy.

Speculating on the future worth of New Orleans issues was a risky proposition. Most of the coins that bear the mark of the O-Mint were genuinely scarce in 1947, but became common once the Treasury opened the vault holding most of the "Creole" dollars in 1962. Of the issues in this tier, 20 are from New Orleans, and of those, 9 are worth no more today in MS-63 than they were in inflation-adjusted dollars in 1947.

There are exceptions.

The 1895-O, of course, became one of the series' key issues. An MS-63 example today is worth nearly $50,000. While not as dramatic, the 1894-O and 1896-O aren't regularly found in Mint State and are elusive in MS-63 and above. Both issues are worth several thousand dollars.

Six Carson City issues make the cut. They are, in sequential order: 1879-CC, 1880-CC, 1881-CC, 1885-CC, 1889-CC, 1892-CC, and 1893-CC.

The 1889-CC was found predominantly in circulated grades. The issue was one of the needle-in-a-haystack offerings of the GSA hoard, with one example discovered in its Mixed CC lots. The 1892-CC and 1893-CC, both rare, were also represented in the GSA by single Uncirculated examples.

All of the San Francisco releases remain desirable, although the big winners are the 1892-S, 1884-S, and 1895-S.

Three circulation-strike Morgan dollars exceeded $15.00 in the 1947 *Red Book*. They were the 1903-S ($45), the 1893-S ($100), and the 1903-O ($110). In inflation-adjusted dollars, the 1903-S would have cost approximately $471 if you could find a truly Uncirculated example. An MS-63 example today will run you about $6,500. That's a 4.06 percent compound annual growth rate. A great buy, but a collector could have done better with any number of investments.

The 1893-S, on the other hand, would have set a collector back $1,047, inflation-adjusted, in 1947. A truly rare piece, only

Scarce-Tier Morgan Dollars (1947 *Red Book*)—$7.50 to $15.00							
$7.50	**$8.50**	**$9.00–$10.00**	**$11.00**	**$12.00**	**$12.50**	**$13.50**	**$15.00**
1879-CC	1887-O	1879-O	1885-S	1884-S	1885-CC	1893-CC	1892-S
1880-O	1897-O	1881-CC	1895-S		1893-O	1895-O	1896-S
1880-CC	1898-O	1888-O	1904-O				
1881-O	1901-S	1891-O					
1882-O	1902-S	1892-CC					
1886-O		1894-S					
1889-O		1901-O					
1889-CC		1902-O					
1892-O							
1896-O							
1899-O							
1900-O							

a handful are even known today in Mint State. Sliders would have abounded in the days before third-party grading. Still, the lucky buyer who picked up an MS-62 example (the grade in which the issue is most likely found in Uncirculated condition) would have realized an annual return of 78 percent if they held the coin through to the present.

Which brings us to the 1903-O, the most expensive Morgan dollar circulation strike in the first edition of the *Red Book*. It's not exactly clear how many verifiably Uncirculated exam-ples were known in the first half of the 20th century. It was cer-tainly considered a rare, if not the rarest, Morgan dollar issue before a massive run-up on the coin elevated it to its peak value of $1,500 ($11,590 adjusted) in 1962. Then, in the fall of that year, hundreds of thousands if not millions of 1903-Os—as well as a huge cache of other New Orleans dollar bags—were re-leased at face value. Speculators made a mad dash to sell the coins at huge profits, while word about the release spread like wildfire through dealer channels. Within a year, the dollar was trading for under $7 a coin.

It remains one of several common-date Morgans.

Rare-Tier Morgan Dollars (1947 *Red Book*)—$45.00 to $110.00		
$45.00	$100.00	$110.00
1903-S	1893-S	1903-O

26th-Edition *Red Book*

Comparing the Morgan dollar market of 1973 to the market of 1947 is a bit like compar-ing apples to oranges, but for our purposes it illustrates the Morgan dollar market at a point when the collector landscape in terms of rare dates released by the Treasury was mostly known. It is also a pivot point for the series, as several market-changing innovations started to surface shortly after the publication of this edition.

The Top Five Morgan Dollar Issues, 1947 vs. 197							
1947				1973			
Rank	Issue	Price	Inflation Adjusted	Rank	Issue	Price	Inflation Adjusted
1.	1903-O	$110	$1,317	1.	1893-S	$5,750	$32,120
2.	1893-S	$100	$1,197	2.	1892-S	$2,900	$16,200
3.	1903-S	$45	$538	3.	1889-CC	$1,000	$5,259
4.	1892-S	$15	$180	4.	1895-S	$560	$3,128
4.	1896-S	$15	$180	5.	1895-O	$525	$2,932
6.	1893-CC	$13.50	$141.36	6.	1903-S	$400	$2,234
7.	1895-O	$13.50	$141.36	7.	1893-O	$250	$1,314
8.	1885-CC	$12.50	$130.89	8.	1893-CC	$240	$1,262
9.	1893-O	$12.50	$130.89	9.	1876-S	$235	$1,236
10.	1884-S	$12.00	$125.65	10.	1879-CC	$225	$1,183
				10.	1894	$225	$1,183

The authors' essay on the Morgan dollar market provided readers in the 1970s with an overview of the price increases each issue in the series had experienced over the course of 25 years. To modern researchers, the 1973 edition shows the Morgan dollar market in transition. For several issues, this time period was the last chance to buy truly valuable coins at inexpensive prices.

The first thing you notice when comparing the 10 most expensive dates from the two *Red Book* editions is that the price of each of the top 10 Morgan dollars increased substantially.

Most of the issues present in the 1947 list remained at or near the top, but three issues dropped off the list by 1973. They are the 1903-O, the 1885-CC, and the 1884-S. The 1885-CC was being offered by the GSA at the time of the 26th edition.

Taking their places were three new additions. In third place was the 1895-S, and tied for ninth were the 1879-CC and the 1894. In total, the 1973 top 10 consists of five San Francisco issues, two Carson City and New Orleans issues, and one Philadelphia release.

The most valuable Morgan dollar issue in 1973 was the 1893-S. No massive stockpiles of 1893-S bags were discovered in the Treasury hoard, which put added pressure on an already sparse surviving population of Mint State pieces. The $5,750 going rate in 1973 was merely a precursor of things to come. As of this writing, the 1893-S in Mint State brings well over $100,000 at auction.

Trailing the 1893-S is the San Francisco issue of 1892. The 1892-S had moved up two spots since 1947, catapulting over the 1903-S. A very difficult coin to obtain in Mint State, the 1892-S also brings six-figure prices at auction in today's market.

The two Carson City issues listed—the 1879-CC and the 1893-CC—were both represented in the GSA hoard. Collectors could mail a bid for one of 3,608 Uncirculated 1879-CC dollars in the February 1974 sale. The GSA-set minimum write-in bid was $300. Demand for the issue was so high that the coins sold for well over that. According to Van Allen and Mallis, the average winning bid for the piece was $478.[1]

Two New Orleans issues carried over: the 1893-O and the 1895-O, neither of which were well represented in the "Creole" dollar releases. The sole Philadelphia issue to make the list—the 1894—has the lowest mintage of any circulation-strike Morgan dollar.

Increased demand for Morgan dollars was felt throughout the series, even though enough material was available that prices were only marginally higher for many common-date Morgans. Adjusted for inflation, common-date coins sold for between $26.18 and $41.88 each. In 1973, the base rate had risen slightly, to $5.00 and $8.00, or $26.30 to $44.70 adjusted.

After 1973, most of the issues in this table continued to inch forward in price, but the 1878, 7 Tail Feathers, and the 1879-O outpaced expectations.

One of the more intriguing facets of the Morgan dollar series is how long it took for the stock of issues not known to be

Common-Tier Morgan Dollars (1973 *Red Book*)—$5.00 to $9.50					
$5.00	$5.25	$5.50–$5.75	$6.00–$6.50	$7.00–$7.25	$8.00–$9.50
1878-S	1879	$5.50	$6.00	$7.00	$8.50
1882	1879-S	1898-O	1880-S	1880-O	1879-O
1882-O	1883	1904-O	1890		
1882-S	1884		1898	$7.25	$8.75
1883-O	1888-O	$5.75		1878 7TF	1903
1884-O	1899-O	1880	$6.50	1897	
1885	1900		1887-O		$9.50
1885-O	1900-O		1921-D		1890-S
1886	1901-O		1921-S		
1887					
1888					
1889					
1896					
1902-O					
1921					

rare to start to dry up. In 1973, one could still buy an 1883-S for $50—a coin that today is worth $5,000 or more in Mint State. One could also buy an 1886-O for $20; now, it's worth more than $3,500 in certified MS-63. The owner of any of the issues in the above chart comes out ahead in today's market.

While scarce dates experienced a solid appreciation in value, many of today's great rarities continued to lurk among more common releases. The 1897-O, 1893, 1892-CC, 1896-O, and 1894-O all trade for more than a thousand dollars in Mint State now, and all of these traded for under $100 in 1973. The 1884-S, at just $100, is a $35,000 coin in MS-63 in today's market. Few issues in the table above underperformed.

While the 1903-S and the 1895-S eventually slipped down a few spots, four of the top six 1973 Morgan dollars retain a high position in the series today. None of these issues were particularly available at any point in the 20th century (most dealers never had them in inventory), but demand was so light in the first half of the 20th century that few realized how much future

Semi-Scarce-Tier Morgan Dollars (1973)—$51 to $250			
$51–$99	$100–$199	$200–$250	$251–$560
$53 1897-O	$100 1884-S 1901	$220 1904-S	$400 1903-O
$55 1901-S	$105 1902-S	$225 1879-CC 1894	$525 1895-O
$65 1894-S		$235 1896-S	$560 1895-S
$67.50 1885-CC		$240 1893-CC	
$68 1893		$250 1893-O	
$70 1880-CC 1892-CC			
$80 1896-O			
$85 1894-O			

Semi-Common-Tier Morgan Dollars (1973 *Red Book*)—$11.00 to $50			
$11.00–$18.00	$19.00–$30.00	$31.00–$40.00	$41.00–$50.00
$11.00 1902	$19.50 1887-S	$31.00 1891-CC	$42.00 1888-S
$14.00 1891	$20.00 1886-O	$34.00 1890-CC	$43.00 1884-CC 1899-S
$15.00 1878 8TF 1891-S 1897-S	$22.00 1904	$35.00 1883-CC 1892 1898-S	$50.00 1883-S
$16.00 1889-O	$28.00 1892-O	$36.50 1900-S	
$16.50 1890-O	$30.00 1899	$40.00 1882-CC 1886-S 1889-S 1903-O	
$17.50 1878-CC 1891-O			
$18.00 1885-S			

interest in the series would put pressure on the scant supply.

In summary, while the 1973 *Red Book* price list shows great maturity in the series, several coins with tremendous upside remained hidden among lesser pieces. As the market shifted in the late 1970s and early 1980s, these coins would provide series experts ample opportunity to cash in. For as big as the Morgan dollar market had become, its true impact on numismatics had not been felt yet.

Miller

The next big shift in the market was a reaction to the Morgan dollar's growing popularity. If abundance made the series popular, then *quality* would separate the run-of-the-mill from the exceptional.

Rare-Tier Morgan Dollars (1973 *Red Book*)—$400 and up			
$400	**$525–$560**	**$1,000– $3,000**	**$5,750**
1903-S	$525 1895-O	$1,000 1889-CC	1893-S
	$560 1895-S	$2,900 1892-S	

Montana dealer Wayne Miller was one of the pioneers of this movement. Starting in 1968 with the help of Dean Tavenner, John B. Love, and other silver-dollar dealers, Miller set out to assemble the highest-quality Morgan dollar set ever built. He spent more than 16 years building his set, which included circulation strikes, Proofs, and certain of the elusive branch-mint Proofs. A majority of the pieces he collected were the finest known at the time.

While he was putting it all together, Miller was very particular about which coins he'd allow in his set. In 1992, he wrote:

During the early years of the project many people laughed when they realized that the set was missing many pieces. 'How can you call this a dollar set? Where's the '89-CC? Where's the '93-CC?' But I was determined early on that I would never put a coin in the set unless there was a reasonable assessment that this was the finest specimen that I was likely to see.[2]

To do this, Miller had to rely on his own skill and judgment since there was no condition census for the Morgan dollar series at this time.

But he did have some advantages. He had little in the way of competition for the best coins, and dealers knew Miller would pay top dollar for high-quality pieces. There was still a tremendous amount of fresh material out there, and being a traveling coin dealer allowed him to go where those coins were. He also happened to live in the heart of "Silver Dollar Country"— Helena, Montana.

Still, this was a new trail Miller and other quality-conscious collectors were blazing. While the Morgan dollar market had been growing year after year, no one other than Miller was paying 10 times *Coin Dealer Newsletter* bid for certain coins. Furthermore, Mint State grading was still in its infancy; most dealers relied on adjectives like *choice* and *gem* to describe the quality of a coin. And while an honest dealer could count on getting premium money for "gem"-quality examples, the premiums were small compared to today's market.

With no sophisticated price guide to go by for top-tier material, Miller based his purchase price on what he thought he had to pay to get the best coins.

The way Miller figured it, an extraordinary example of a New Orleans issue that's usually flat struck and unappealing was worth more than a mediocre coin from a rare date. This approach ran contrary to what many collectors agreed was the "correct" way to collect—to focus on rare issues above all else. Guided by such orthodoxy, who would collect a series as readily accessible as the Morgan dollar? Such thinking left the series dormant for more than 60 years.

What Miller's approach did was create a new blueprint for the industry. It didn't just show dealers and collectors how to proceed and profit from selling the Morgan dollar, it showed them how to grow the hobby by more thoughtfully considering the inventory on hand. Premium coins, regardless of their origins, are worth premium money to the right buyer. As it turned out, Miller was right, and many other collectors quickly followed suit. And not just with Morgan dollars, but other series as well.

It's been 30 years since the Miller collection was offered for sale in the high-profile Superior Galleries Hoagy Carmichael and Wayne Miller Auction.[3] Miller attended with his beautiful wife, Ann, but he wasn't there merely to observe. He was there to win some coins back. This raised a few eyebrows among the other bidders, who didn't know Miller had sold his set to a high-profile California collector two years prior. David Hall was the purchasing agent for that transaction.

The auction proved to be a turning point for the Morgan dollar series. Later that year, Professional Coin Grading Service debuted and the rest, as they say, is history.

Enter the Set Registry and Miller Reconsidered

On August 9, 1989, PCGS founder David Hall and legendary collector John J. Ford sat on a panel at the American Numismatic Association convention in Pittsburgh, Pennsylvania.[4] The topic? Coin grading. Ford, representing the old guard, railed against the hobby's newfound reliance on grading and pointed to a developing schism between the collector and investor markets. Ford felt that ignorant investors were being duped by clever marketing, and that third-party grading overemphasized grade at the expense of rarity, historical association, and provenance. For a man who had spent his entire career in and around the coin business, and amassed one of the most significant collections of all time, these were serious allegations.

But Hall stood his ground, saying that in the coin market, like every other collectibles market, "quality always commands a premium price." Hall was right, of course; better coins brought more excitement at auctions, at coin shows, and retail shops. The Sheldon scale, the system on which coin grading was loosely based, ties value to condition. What Hall had done was provide the hobby a means with which to grant liquidity to quality based on four pillars: unbiased and conservative grading, tamperproof holders, a buy-back guarantee, and statistical tables tracking every coin graded in each grade.

This simple approach changed the face of numismatics, and whether Ford liked it or not there was no turning back.

I bring this up because Wayne Miller had none of the tools that David Hall's PCGS offered collectors when he built his amazing set. He nonetheless sought out the best-quality coins and paid top dollar for them when the market forced him to, though it helped his checkbook that the high-end collectibles market had not yet fully matured.

What Miller did without the benefits of third-party grading boggles the mind, but it demonstrates how many more advantages collectors have now than in the 1970s and early 1980s. Finicky collectors no longer need to pick through thousands of coins (sometimes literally) to find a piece that fits their needs. Quality always commands a premium, but at least now the market has a more efficient way of filtering for it.

But PCGS wasn't done.

In 1992, the company launched Set Registry, a radical innovation that allowed collectors to pit their sets against others in a worldwide

competition to put together the best set. PCGS created two leaderboards, one for current sets and the other for all-time sets. This allowed participants to see how their sets stacked up against some of the most notable sets in the history of the hobby.

Since its launch, the PCGS Set Registry has grown to contain thousands of possible set types, with collectors listing more than 60,000 registered sets.

Set construction followed a logical progression, from basic to advanced. PCGS developed templates for 32 sets that cover the Morgan dollar series. The most popular sets are as follows:

> Morgan Dollar Date Set, Circulation Strikes—requires one issue per date for the series' entire run.
>
> Morgan Dollar Basic Set, Circulation Strikes—requires each issue from the series.
>
> Morgan Dollar Super Set—requires a coin from each issue in the series plus more than 100 VAM varieties (a daunting challenge for even the most sophisticated dollar collector).

For most set types, PCGS employs a weighting system in favor of scarcer issues. In the Morgan Dollar Basic Set, for example, the most difficult issues to obtain are given a weighted value of 10, while the easiest ones are assigned a value of 1. The 1886, being a common-date coin, is assigned a value of 1 and is therefore worth its grade.

The table below illustrates this point.

Date	Grade	Weight	Weighted Value
1886	67	1	67
1886-O	65	8	520
1886-S	65	6	390
Total Coins: 3	Weighted GPA: 65.13		

In the above example, the collector has a common 1886 in the impressive grade of MS-67, and the two scarcer New Orleans and San Francisco 1886 issues in MS-65.

Miller pieced together his set without the convenience of population reports, without the benefit of 24-hour access to online auctions, or even a proven premium market for the coin. Miller had no other high-end Morgan dollar sets with which to compare his. And while he did a fantastic job of evaluating the coins he ultimately included in his set, he had no way of knowing—on a date-by-date, mint-by-mint basis—whether he had in fact purchased the best example of the issue in existence.

In essence, Miller was confirming a premium market for the series and doing so without a safety net. His success in putting together a world-class Morgan dollar collection and the successive releases of high-profile Morgan dollar hoards meant that Miller would not just be a pioneering collector in a great series, but one of the key progenitors of the modern-day Morgan dollar market.

But was it yet possible for Miller to put together the all-time-best Morgan dollar collection when he set out to do it?

Nowadays, thanks to the recordkeeping of major grading services like PCGS, collectors have a more complete idea of the rank of a coin, based on grade, relative to all other coins from that issue that have been graded. This wasn't possible overnight. It took more than 30 years of grading hundreds of thousands of coins.

Today's collector has more sophisticated tools that can be utilized to know up-to-date coin populations in the Mint State grades to within half a point. We can see a robust accounting of previous public auctions, view high-resolution images of particular coins, and evaluate purchases based on how much they help a set using PCGS's free-to-use online Set Registry product.

These tools by no means take all of the skill out of collecting. No two coins are exactly alike, which means even coins in the same grade can have different values in the marketplace. In some instances, it takes an experienced numismatist to see the differences between similarly graded coins. And it takes a real understanding of the market to determine a coin's potential. This was true during Miller's time, when he was paying 10 times bid for a coin he really liked, and it is true now.

So how did Miller do? PCGS assigns estimated grades to Miller's set coins. According to this calculation, the Wayne Miller set ranks 42nd in the All-Time Finest List of Morgan Dollar Basic Set, Circulation Strikes (1878–1921). PCGS's ranking omits Miller's 1885-P and 1893-S. With those coins, his set would likely rank in the top 15.

Miller's 1893-S was the first MS-65 of this issue graded by PCGS—I personally submitted the coin for grading. Miller did not have the coin at the time his set was sold at auction, however, and this is why it is not included on PCGS's reconstruction of his set.

According to PCGS's inferences, the Miller set contained 14 issues where no finer coin is known, 6 issues where only one better example is known, and 14 issues where between two and five better examples are known. So for at least 34 of the 97 pieces in the set, Miller had acquired the best or nearly the best possible example.

The Miller set does have its weaknesses, however. His 1882-S, which he called a "sleeper" in his groundbreaking book

An Analysis of Morgan and Peace Dollars (1976), has been bettered by more than 5,000 coins over the span of three higher grade points. The 1882-CC, a coin that Miller felt was overpriced after the release of the GSA hoard, was likewise bettered by three points, with more than 1,300 coins grading higher. The same story plays out, more or less, with about a dozen issues. Had Miller been able to pursue his set with all of the conveniences of the modern age, one has to believe that he would have shored up these deficiencies.

In the years since Miller's set was sold and broken up, several Morgan dollar collectors have surpassed this early effort. The members of this exclusive club read like a who's-who of dollar-set builders: Jack Lee (first and foremost), George Bodway, Mike Casper, Ray Cassano, Mike Gilley, John Highfill, Monty Wiener, and Sacramento lumber-store magnate Lloyd Gabbert.

The prices of the premier coins have also risen precipitously. Top-tier collectors know putting together an elite Morgan dollar set is not so much a challenge of discovery (assuming that most, if not all, of the best-preserved Morgan dollars are known to the market by now), but more of an expensive and intricate jigsaw puzzle, where the value of each piece correlates with what it can and can't do to help grow the set.

The market for these premium coins at top dollar may be limited to the number of active high-profile buyers in the market at any given time, but the appeal of high-end coins goes far beyond a handful of major collectors. What mainstream collector wouldn't want a common-date 1881-S Morgan dollar in a high grade? And so it goes. Demand for the best available on the market drives prices upwards at all levels in Mint State—buoyed by the ease of access to knowledge that collectors now have, which tells them how any given piece relates to others in any given series, for any given date, from any given mint.

A detail of "Silver Dollars," from the southeast side of 100 Second Avenue North, in Nashville's commercial district.
(From the Library of Congress's "Historic American Buildings Survey")

Chapter Four

Year-by-Year Breakdown

This chapter explores each Morgan dollar by date and mintmark. It covers circulation-strike coins plus one Proof (the 1895) that traditionally has been collected with the circulation-strike series. (Proofs are further discussed in chapter 5.) Information on each coin includes its mintage; certified population (number of PCGS grading events, which may include multiple submissions for individual coins); the percentages of prooflike and deep mirror prooflike coins; historical narrative; and detailed certification and value tables. The price guide reflects retail prices for slabbed (professionally graded, as opposed to "raw" or unslabbed) coins. Full-coin photographs in this chapter are of coins from the Coronet Collection.

1878, 8TF (Eight Tail Feathers)

Mintage . . . . 699,300[1] or 749,500[2]

Certified Population . . . . 15,033[3]

Prooflike % 6.29

Deep Mirror Prooflike % 1.64

The story of the Morgan dollar begins with the 1878 8TF or Eight Tail Feathers variety. Struck in Philadelphia, the 8TF was the design that Mint director Dr. Henry R. Linderman approved after a period of several months spent experimenting with and revising Assistant Engraver George T. Morgan's design.

The Mint had been preparing for the coin's release for more than a year before the enacting legislation was even authorized. In fact, the English-born Morgan was recruited from the London Mint in order to satisfy Linderman's desire to elevate the aesthetic quality of American coins, something he didn't think his current team of engravers (including the father-and-son team of William and Charles Barber) was capable of doing.

On March 11, 1878, not quite two weeks after the passage of the Bland-Allison Act, the first specimen-strike Morgan dollars were produced using Linderman's approved designs.

The first coin was given to the president of the United States, Rutherford B. Hayes, who had vetoed the Act just months earlier. Congress had overridden his veto on February 28.

The 1878 8TF comprises less than 10 percent of Philadelphia's total output for the year. The typical Uncirculated coin grades MS-62 to MS-64, with gem-quality coins being readily available. Prooflike coins make up 6.3 percent of PCGS's total graded population. Deep mirror prooflike examples are elusive.

Interesting fact: The 1878 8TF has a slightly higher relief than Morgan dollars struck with the revised 7TF reverse.

1878, 8TF
Certified Populations and Check List
Mint State

Circ	MS-60	MS-61	MS-62	MS-63	MS-64	MS-65	MS-66	MS-67	MS-68
1,150	122	544	2,561	4,523	2,772	567	34	2	1

Prooflike

Circ	MS-60	MS-61	MS-62	MS-63	MS-64	MS-65	MS-66	MS-67	MS-68
1	24	79	278	296	146	14			

Deep Mirror Prooflike

Circ	MS-60	MS-61	MS-62	MS-63	MS-64	MS-65	MS-66	MS-67	MS-68
	6	24	67	74	43	4	1		

1878, 7/8 TF (Seven Over Eight Tail Feathers), Strong and Weak

Strong.

Weak.

Mintage . . . . 544,000 [4]

Certified Population. 7,508

Prooflike % 4.53

Deep Mirror Prooflike %. 2.22

On March 18, Mint Director Henry Linderman met with officials and members of the engraving department to discuss his concerns about the slow rate of die production. The Bland-Allison Act compelled the Mint to coin an unprecedented number of silver dollars per month, and in order to do this the Mother Mint needed to expedite the shipment of dies and collars to the branch mints at Carson City and San Francisco so that they could put their production capacity to good use.

In correspondence with Chief Engraver William Barber, it was brought to Linderman's attention that special processes had to be undertaken to basin the dies, and that the staff of the Philadelphia Mint felt the branch mints were not up to the task.[5] Changes had to be made to the coin.

The key change that collectors note is the reduction of the number of tail feathers from eight to seven, a seemingly frivolous alteration, which according to numismatic lore was brought about by Linderman's citation of prior precedents. A quick review of American heraldic eagles debunks this theory.

More importantly for the production of dies, Linderman ordered a slight lowering of the relief. This made it easier for the Philadelphia die shop to produce enough dies to serve the branch mints, which then struck up 11.9 million Morgan dollars in addition to Philadelphia's 10.5 million.

But what to do with the dies already finished? Instead of discarding them, the engraving team imparted the newly mandated seven tail feathers over the old design. The handiwork is evident, as each of the dies can be individuated by trained numismatists. This is why we have the 1878, 7 Over 8 Tail Feather family of varieties.

PCGS splits the 1878 7/8 TF varieties into two categories: Strong and Weak. The 1878 7/8 TF Strong features prominently visible tail feathers underneath the superimposed image. The Weak variety, as the name implies, shows some of the 8TF image but not as much. Collectors tend to prefer examples where the underlying feathers are more visible; therefore the Strong variety commands a higher price.

The typical grade of the 1878 7/8 TF Strong is on par with the 1878 8TF. The typical Uncirculated grade of this issue is from MS-62 to MS-64. Prooflike and deep mirror prooflike coins, while scarce, are typically found in MS-63. Attractive DMPLs are as elusive as the 1878 8TF.

1878, 7/8 TF, Strong
Certified Populations and Check List
Mint State

Circ	MS-60	MS-61	MS-62	MS-63	MS-64	MS-65	MS-66	MS-67	MS-68
291	58	279	1,338	2,635	1,584	267	6		

Prooflike

Circ	MS-60	MS-61	MS-62	MS-63	MS-64	MS-65	MS-66	MS-67	MS-68
	8	21	89	116	72	8			

Deep Mirror Prooflike

Circ	MS-60	MS-61	MS-62	MS-63	MS-64	MS-65	MS-66	MS-67	MS-68
	5	16	40	49	41	3	1		

1878, 7/8 TF, Weak
Certified Populations and Check List
Mint State

Circ	MS-60	MS-61	MS-62	MS-63	MS-64	MS-65	MS-66	MS-67	MS-68
97	12	76	557	1,171	797	117	7		

Prooflike

Circ	MS-60	MS-61	MS-62	MS-63	MS-64	MS-65	MS-66	MS-67	MS-68
	4	7	29	50	21	4			

Deep Mirror Prooflike

Circ	MS-60	MS-61	MS-62	MS-63	MS-64	MS-65	MS-66	MS-67	MS-68
		7	23	43	32	4			

1878, 7 TF (Seven Tail Feathers)

Reverse of 1878.

Reverse of 1879.

	7TF, Reverse of 1878	7TF, Reverse of 1879
Mintage	4,900,000 (Breen); 7,200,000 (Bowers); 7,000,000 (Miller)	4,300,000 (Breen); 2,000,000 (Miller and Bowers)
Certified Population	16,951	6,003
Prooflike %	6.78	3.20
Deep Mirror Prooflike %	3.1	1.8

The engravers at the Philadelphia Mint fulfilled Director Henry Linderman's directive to make certain alterations to the Morgan dollar design, first by superimposition of the 7TF design element and then by preparing new dies by the start of April. Once Linderman was satisfied with the coin, dies earmarked for the branch mints were packaged and dispatched, while Philadelphia began production of the slightly-lowered-relief 7TF Morgan dollar.

From April through the end of the year, Philadelphia's output of 7TF Morgans exceeded 9.75 million coins, putting the total output of P-Mint Morgans in excess of 10.5 million coins.

There are two major die varieties of the 1878 7TF reverse:

The first, known as the reverse of 1878, features a flat-breasted eagle, seven tail feathers, and parallel arrow feathers.

The second variety—the reverse of 1879—gained visibility in the 1970s and 1980s. It features an angled top arrow feather, seven tail feathers, and a rounded eagle's chest. There are other slight differences, but these naked-eye pick-ups are rela-tively easy to spot. This is the reverse design predominantly used in the coin's second year of production.

The exact population dispersal of the two varieties isn't known to any degree of specificity. It is assumed that the reverse of 1879 came into production later and is less common than the reverse of 1878. There is a slight premium for Reverse of 1879 issues in most grades, and pronounced premiums in the higher-grade registry.

Prooflike and deep mirror prooflike examples of the 7TF Reverse of '78 variety are more widely available than any of the other P-Mint 1878 issues. The scarcer 7TF Reverse of '79 variety is the equally scarce in PL and DMPL.

1878, 7TF, Reverse of 1878
Certified Populations and Check List
Mint State

Circ	MS-60	MS-61	MS-62	MS-63	MS-64	MS-65	MS-66	MS-67	MS-68
1,654	78	543	2,936	5,695	3,663	666	40		

Prooflike

Circ	MS-60	MS-61	MS-62	MS-63	MS-64	MS-65	MS-66	MS-67	MS-68
1	14	77	313	470	230	41	3		

Deep Mirror Prooflike

Circ	MS-60	MS-61	MS-62	MS-63	MS-64	MS-65	MS-66	MS-67	MS-68
	11	34	125	217	119	21			

1878, 7TF, Reverse of 1879
Certified Populations and Check List
Mint State

Circ	MS-60	MS-61	MS-62	MS-63	MS-64	MS-65	MS-66	MS-67	MS-68
753	66	223	1,064	1,880	1,321	382	13		

Prooflike

Circ	MS-60	MS-61	MS-62	MS-63	MS-64	MS-65	MS-66	MS-67	MS-68
	5	15	48	80	38	5	1		

Deep Mirror Prooflike

Circ	MS-60	MS-61	MS-62	MS-63	MS-64	MS-65	MS-66	MS-67	MS-68
	3	9	24	44	24	5			

1878-CC

Mintage 2,212,000

Certified Population 25,400

Prooflike % 6.25

Deep Mirror Prooflike % 1.59

Once the Philadelphia Mint was able to create modified 7TF dies of sufficient hardiness, shipments of dies earmarked for Carson City and San Francisco began. Mint records show that the first Carson City dies left Philadelphia on April 8, almost one month after coining of the new dollar began. They arrived at the Nevada mint on April 16.

The mint at Carson City resembled a fortress constructed out of sandstone, and stood at the foot of the Sierra Nevada Mountains along a strip of hastily constructed wooden buildings on the city's main thoroughfare. Its architectural style was significant in that it shaped area design for decades and continues to serve as the symbol of the state's historic past as a museum located in the heart of Nevada's capital.

The Carson City Mint, like the Charlotte and Dahlonega mints before it, was constructed not in a burgeoning American city, but in close proximity to bullion reserves in the midst of great mining operations. The CC Mint struck its first coins in 1870, and produced a small volume of Liberty Seated dollars before the Coinage Act of 1873 abolished the program.

Even though the Carson City Mint was located near the epicenter of such a large mining enterprise, it was the least profitable of all of the branch mints. The mint's remote location and rugged environment certainly were factors, as was corruption in the supply chain and delivery system, and the need for additional security in handling and transporting struck coinage and deposited bullion. Because of this, there was always a clamor to

shut the facility down. In fact, much to the dismay of Congress and the Treasury Department, it was actually cheaper to ship bullion to San Francisco and ship the coins inland.

Nevertheless, the Morgan dollars of the Carson City Mint would go on to play a huge role in the numismatic revival of the series, as the mystique of the Old West gives CC Mint dollars a unique allure for coin collectors and non-collectors alike.

Of the 2.9 million dollars that comprised the GSA hoard, only 61,000 were from the 1878-CC issue, which is just 2.7 percent of the mintage. As of 2013, PCGS had graded almost a third of that number in Mint State. Still, there's no shortage of demand for the issue, with premium examples bringing the most money.

The typical 1878-CC dollar as found today grades MS-62 to 64, with gem or better coins being uncommon and quite scarce in MS-66. Collector demand for the coin is generally greater than the total number of coins certified by PCGS. The percentage of prooflike and deep mirror prooflike coins is on par for the rest of the 1878 issues.

1878-CC
Certified Populations and Check List
Mint State

Circ	MS-60	MS-61	MS-62	MS-63	MS-64	MS-65	MS-66	MS-67	MS-68
2,423	222	780	3,719	7,995	6,339	1,701	224	5	

Prooflike

Circ	MS-60	MS-61	MS-62	MS-63	MS-64	MS-65	MS-66	MS-67	MS-68
	28	89	342	551	449	119	10		

Deep Mirror Prooflike

Circ	MS-60	MS-61	MS-62	MS-63	MS-64	MS-65	MS-66	MS-67	MS-68
	6	16	67	161	119	32	3		

1878-S

Mintage 9,774,000

Certified Population. 39,031

Prooflike % 3.51

Deep Mirror Prooflike %. 0.59

The California Gold Rush of 1848 to 1855 offered thousands of Americans new hope for economic prosperity. Tens of thousands flocked to the coastal territories looking for gold and a chance at a new life. Due in large part to the area's vast resources, California was admitted to the Union as the 31st state on September 9, 1850. That same year, President Millard Fillmore proposed the building of a branch mint in San Francisco to process the massive amounts of gold ore being extracted in California mines. In 1852, Congress authorized Fillmore's plan and began to set up shop in the existing Moffat & Company building.

The San Francisco Mint opened for business in 1854 and quickly got up to speed, minting coins at a rate that sometimes rivaled that of the Philadelphia Mint. By the end of the Civil War it had become obvious that the San Francisco Mint had outgrown its old facilities, and in 1874 mint operations were moved to an impressive new edifice designed by the Treasury Department's supervising architect, Alfred B. Mullett. Mullet had recently finished construction of the Carson City Mint and was simultaneously building an assay office in Boise, Idaho.

The San Francisco Mint, now in a state-of-the-art facility, was an efficient branch mint, which spoke well of the growing prominence of a city that had become the jewel of the American West. Over the course of the Morgan dollar's production period of 1878 to 1921, many of the highest-quality pieces known to collectors would originate here.

For so many 1878-S dollars to have turned out as nicely as they did is a minor miracle, since problems with production began almost immediately. Of the 10 die pairs that were sent to the mint from Philadelphia on April 8, only two pairs were deemed suitable for coining.

To make matters worse, one of the usable dies broke on the first day after striking fewer than than a thousand coins. Fortunately, the San Francisco Mint was able to get the supplies they needed to continue striking dollars and by the end of the year they turned out an impressive total of 9,774,000.

The 1878-S Morgan dollar typically comes well struck and satiny. PCGS has certified nearly 40,000 examples of the issue, and most grade between MS-62 and MS-65.

While the percentage of prooflike or deep mirror prooflike coins looks low compared to the total number of coins graded by PCGS, the actual number of coins with these attributions is on par with the rest of the issues for the date, except for the fact that the quality of this issue tends to be the nicest.

1878-S
Certified Populations and Check List
Mint State

Circ	MS-60	MS-61	MS-62	MS-63	MS-64	MS-65	MS-66	MS-67	MS-68
1,523	134	761	4,659	13,039	13,008	3,672	612	20	1

Prooflike

Circ	MS-60	MS-61	MS-62	MS-63	MS-64	MS-65	MS-66	MS-67	MS-68
	5	50	234	490	453	127	9	0	2

Deep Mirror Prooflike

Circ	MS-60	MS-61	MS-62	MS-63	MS-64	MS-65	MS-66	MS-67	MS-68
	3	12	62	76	60	16	3		

1879

Mintage 14,806,000

Certified Population. 39,031

Prooflike % 2.94

Deep Mirror Prooflike % 1.33

Mandated design changes that occurred mid-production in 1878 did not recur in 1879, but difficulties procuring sufficient amounts of bullion for the branch mints tested Philadelphia's capacity. As it stood, Philadelphia coiners had scant time to strike anything but the legally mandated number of dollar coins and 16 million–plus Indian Head cents (the latter denomination would not be minted elsewhere until 1908).

Nevertheless, the Mint was able to supply its branches with sufficient dies. This included New Orleans, reactivated for the first time since it had been seized by the Confederate government in the opening days of the rebellion. Federal troops had recaptured the facility in early 1862, but it didn't reopen until 1879.

Total dollar production at the Philadelphia Mint increased more than 40 percent, to a total of 14,806,000 coins, all with the same reverse design. Overall quality is on par with the P-Mint issues of 1878. MS-62 through MS-64 is the norm and gems, while not rare, are typically the subjects of strong competition on the part of collectors. After four decades of grading, there are fewer than 500 prooflike and deep mirror prooflike examples certified by PCGS. (As PCGS population figures report *grading events* and not *individual coins*, the actual number of examples is likely some percentage less.)

Change of Address: When George T. Morgan took the job of assistant engraver at the U.S. Mint, he wasn't sure it would work out. By 1879, he was convinced that it would and finally gave up his residence in London. Morgan would continue at the Mint until his death in January 1925. He became chief engraver of the U.S. Mint in 1917.

1879
Certified Populations and Check List
Mint State

Circ	MS-60	MS-61	MS-62	MS-63	MS-64	MS-65	MS-66	MS-67	MS-68
690	47	239	1,401	4,047	3,503	972	120	1	

Prooflike

Circ	MS-60	MS-61	MS-62	MS-63	MS-64	MS-65	MS-66	MS-67	MS-68
	7	30	86	106	91	17	1		

Deep Mirror Prooflike

Circ	MS-60	MS-61	MS-62	MS-63	MS-64	MS-65	MS-66	MS-67	MS-68
	6	25	47	67	66	7	1		

1879-CC

Mintage 756,000

Certified Population. 4,691

Prooflike % 6.22

Deep Mirror Prooflike %. 4.67

The first truly scarce issue of the Morgan dollar series is the 1879-CC. This coveted coin was rare in its own time, with a low mintage due to a lack of silver. Apparently, collusion between greedy silver producers and railroad owners made it cheaper to strike silver dollars in San Francisco than at a branch mint constructed solely for the purpose of coining local bullion. So on February 26, 1879, the order was issued to suspend silver-dollar production at Carson City once that facility used up the bullion it had on hand.[6]

When the GSA offered the 1879-CC as part of its February 1974 sale, the issue was represented by the second-lowest amount of Carson City dollar coins in the hoard (the 1890-CC had 19 fewer). The GSA hoard contained 4,100 examples of this issue, 3,608 of which were offered in that sale. The remaining 492 pieces were deemed of lesser quality and sold in the Mixed CC second, fifth, and sixth sales.

The first batch of high-quality pieces was offered to the public with a minimum bid of $400 per coin, and quickly sold out. Adjusted for inflation, $400 in 1974 is approximately $1,900 in today's money.[7] And while that is a great sum, collectors lucky enough to score an 1879-CC dollar did quite well, as the coin today is worth more than double its inflation-adjusted value in all grades up to MS-63, and more than triple in MS-64!

Prooflike and deep cameo prooflike coins from this issue are extremely scarce, as you'd expect since this issue is scarce to begin with. The distribution of grades for these issues is in line with the average grade for Uncirculated coins in the general population. MS-62 to MS-64 is the expected quality for any surviving 1879-CC Morgan dollar.

To Cap or Uncap: The 1879-CC has an anomalous variety that's actually worth *less* than the regular issue. This variety is known as the 1879-CC Capped Die, or more correctly, the 1879-CC Over CC. As the latter suggests, a large CC mintmark was stamped over an area where the smaller 1878 CC mintmark had been stamped. In an effort to obliterate any evidence of the smaller mintmark on the dies, a rough-looking area was left on the die by Carson City mint engravers. The subsequent large CC mintmark looks blurry by comparison. The 1879-CC Over CC was found to be in both the GSA and Redfield hoards.

1879-CC
Certified Populations and Check List
Mint State

Circ	MS-60	MS-61	MS-62	MS-63	MS-64	MS-65	MS-66	MS-67	MS-68
1,725	64	173	487	759	870	100	2		

Prooflike

Circ	MS-60	MS-61	MS-62	MS-63	MS-64	MS-65	MS-66	MS-67	MS-68
	12	25	74	96	77	8			

Deep Mirror Prooflike

Circ	MS-60	MS-61	MS-62	MS-63	MS-64	MS-65	MS-66	MS-67	MS-68
	6	25	47	67	66	7	1		

1879-O

Mintage	2,887,000
Certified Population	10,716
Prooflike %	2.40
Deep Mirror Prooflike %	1.46

Authorization to build a branch mint in New Orleans was part of the Act of March 3, 1835. The same act authorized the building of the Charlotte and Dahlonega mints as well, in addition to an assay office in New York City. Of the three new mints, New Orleans was the only one not built to handle newly mined domestic bullion; its purpose instead was to re-coin foreign silver and gold into U.S. coin. By the time construction on the mint had finished, New Orleans was the third-largest city in the United States, overtaking Philadelphia and Boston.

When the Civil War broke out in 1861, the Southern branch mints fell into the hands of the rebels. The Confederate New Orleans Mint operated for only a short time before bullion supplies dried up and coining activities were suspended. Union forces recaptured the city and the mint in April 1862.

The building would serve various functions until it was reopened in 1873 as an assay office. It was reinstated as a mint in order to fulfill the requirements of the Bland-Allison Act of 1878. After extensive restoration in the midst of a yellow-fever outbreak that claimed the lives of more than 4,600 people, the New Orleans Mint reopened on February 20, 1879, just six days before the Mint director stopped silver shipments to the Carson City Mint.

New Orleans produced 2,887,000 Morgan dollars in 1879, a number that was tempered only by the mint's ability to source silver bullion. Many coins from the issue were briefly circulated, returning to the Treasury, and stored, which is why we see a great number of About Uncirculated coins. The average Uncirculated example grades from MS-62 to MS-64. Gems are elusive, as are prooflikes and deep mirror prooflikes, which comprise 2.4 percent and 1.46 percent respectively of the overall certified population.

1879-O
Certified Populations and Check List
Mint State

Circ	MS-60	MS-61	MS-62	MS-63	MS-64	MS-65	MS-66	MS-67	MS-68
1,473	234	673	2,350	3,248	2,008	303	14		

Prooflike

Circ	MS-60	MS-61	MS-62	MS-63	MS-64	MS-65	MS-66	MS-67	MS-68
	20	40	56	92	47	2			

Deep Mirror Prooflike

Circ	MS-60	MS-61	MS-62	MS-63	MS-64	MS-65	MS-66	MS-67	MS-68
	7	25	50	41	30	3			

1879-S

	Reverse of 1878	Reverse of 1879
Mintage 9,110,000		
Certified Population..........	3,531	95,544
Prooflike %	1.87	5.00
Deep Mirror Prooflike %.....	0.00	0.88

Reverse of 1878.

Reverse of 1879.

The Morgan dollar represented more than 80 percent of the San Francisco Mint's output in 1879, and that year it was the only coin struck there that wasn't made of gold. San Francisco minted 9.1 million Morgan dollars over the course of the year, creating an issue known for its tremendous quality. After 130-plus years, more than 80 examples of the 1879-S have been certified MS-68 by PCGS, while more than 1,300 grade MS-67! Choice and gem coins are readily available, and even MS-66 examples are easy to come by.

The majority of 1879-S Morgans feature what is referred to as the Reverse of 1879, which is the standard reverse for this year. At some point, coins were produced using dies left over from 1878. It's unknown whether this was a mistake on the part of the San Francisco Mint or a packaging error by the staff of the Philadelphia Mint. The 1879-S, Reverse of 1878, variety is scarce and sells for a significant premium over the more common 1879-S.

This issue was heavily stockpiled by the Treasury Department, with only a low percentage of coins struck entering circulation. The Treasury kept several thousand bags of Uncirculated 1879-S Morgans in their vaults for decades, gradually releasing them throughout the 20th century. The 1879-S was well represented in the Continental-Illinois Bank Hoard, and according to numismatist John Kamin three bags of the 1879-S, Reverse of 1878, were found in the Redfield Hoard.

From Father to Son: Morgan dollar designer George T. Morgan was brought into the U.S. Mint's engraving department and was a bit of an outsider. Not because he was an English expatriate—Chief Engraver William Barber also hailed from England and emigrated to the United States, in 1852, at the age of 45—but because Barber and his son were a formidable two-person team and the younger Barber was determined to take the reins from his father.

That day came sooner than expected after William Barber fell ill during a family vacation at Atlantic City, New Jersey, in August 1879. The elder Barber returned to Philadelphia and died on August 31. Charles was appointed chief engraver of the U.S. Mint that same day.

Morgan stayed on at the Mint and was appointed chief engraver after Charles Barber's death on February 18, 1917.

1879-S, Reverse of 1878 (Scarce)
Certified Populations and Check List
Mint State

Circ	MS-60	MS-61	MS-62	MS-63	MS-64	MS-65	MS-66	MS-67	MS-68
489	245	445	861	810	563	50	2		

Prooflike

Circ	MS-60	MS-61	MS-62	MS-63	MS-64	MS-65	MS-66	MS-67	MS-68
	4	9	17	27	9				

Deep Mirror Prooflike

Circ	MS-60	MS-61	MS-62	MS-63	MS-64	MS-65	MS-66	MS-67	MS-68

1879-S, Reverse of 1879 (Common)
Certified Populations and Check List
Mint State

Circ	MS-60	MS-61	MS-62	MS-63	MS-64	MS-65	MS-66	MS-67	MS-68
287	42	386	3,272	18,900	35,876	22,954	6,829	1,300	84

Prooflike

Circ	MS-60	MS-61	MS-62	MS-63	MS-64	MS-65	MS-66	MS-67	MS-68
	13	54	306	1,195	1,809	1,063	291	44	2

Deep Mirror Prooflike

Circ	MS-60	MS-61	MS-62	MS-63	MS-64	MS-65	MS-66	MS-67	MS-68
	2	13	81	235	303	149	46	8	

1880

Mintage 12,600,000

Certified Population. 12,114

Prooflike % 2.00

Deep Mirror Prooflike %. 1.61

With a population of more than 50 million coins, silver supporters expected that the new dollar coin would circulate easily, but by 1880 a majority of Morgan dollars struck were sitting in government vaults across the country. By the end of the year, there would be one new dollar coin for every man, woman, and child in the United States of America.

For its part, the Philadelphia Mint continued to comply with the law. It struck 12.6 million dollar coins, a slight decline from 1879. Ramped-up production in New Orleans had lessened the burden on the Mother Mint.

1880-P coins were preserved in Mint bags for decades, meaning a majority of them never circulated. The coin was readily available throughout the 20th century in Uncirculated grades, with multiple bags being released in the 1940s, 1950s, and early 1960s. Today, nearly all of the bags have been opened and all of the coins dispersed.

The average 1880 Morgan dollar is reasonably well struck with nice luster, grading from MS-62 to MS-64. The large size of the coin makes finding gems a challenge; prooflike and deep mirror prooflike coins are particularly scarce for this issue.

Pastoral Americana: From laborers in the orchards and dairy farms of Adams County, Pennsylvania, to the olive farmers and small-time fishermen working off of the golden coast of California, in 1880 about one third of the nation's workforce were immigrants and more than one half of the country's working population—including children—were employed in agriculture. The average weekly wage of a common laborer, working 10 hours a day, six days a week, was just over $8.

1880
Certified Populations and Check List
Mint State

Circ	MS-60	MS-61	MS-62	MS-63	MS-64	MS-65	MS-66	MS-67	MS-68
782	59	246	1,396	4,246	3,873	960	115		

Prooflike

Circ	MS-60	MS-61	MS-62	MS-63	MS-64	MS-65	MS-66	MS-67	MS-68
	1	5	54	65	96	19	2		

Deep Mirror Prooflike

Circ	MS-60	MS-61	MS-62	MS-63	MS-64	MS-65	MS-66	MS-67	MS-68
		7	17	53	87	30	1		

1880-CC

Mintage	495,000 (net)
Certified Population	13,376
Prooflike %	5.94
Deep Mirror Prooflike %	1.57

The bullion shortage that plagued the Carson City Mint in 1879 continued through the first half of 1880. It wasn't until the first of May that the beleaguered mint had enough bullion to resume coinage operations. In the remaining eight months, the CC Mint struck 51,407 half eagles, 11,190 eagles, and a paltry 591,000 dollar coins—roughly the equivalent to a light month in Philadelphia. Hardly what one would expect from a mint located in the heart of mining country.

Of the 591,000 dollar coins struck, some 96,000 failed to meet legal standards when Mint assayers surveyed Carson City's output. These coins were melted. A majority of the remainder was stored in mint vaults until 1933, when the assay office at the Carson City facility was closed and the Treasury Department ordered the coins shipped to Treasury vaults in Washington, D.C.

Numismatists have many varieties to consider when looking at the 1880-CC. For starters, there is the 1880-CC with the 1878 7TF Parallel Arrow Feather reverse, which accounts for approximately 20 percent of the issue's total mintage. There are also a number of overdates for the 1878 7TF, which are paired with 1878 and 1879 reverses.

Treasury holdings of the 1880-CC issue totaled 131,529 coins, or 26.5 percent of the net mintage. The coins were offered in the third GSA sale, which started in October 1973, and then again at the fifth sale, which began in April 1974. For both offerings the minimum bid per coin was $60.

The final GSA sale of Uncirculated 1880-CC dollars was scheduled to take place in early 1980. This plan was scrapped, however, due to the run-up on silver bullion prices caused by the attempts of Nelson and William Hunt, two billionaire oil tycoons from Texas, to corner the global silver market. Silver's rise and the Hunt Brothers' good fortune would come to a cashing end on March 27, 1980, a day known as "Silver Thursday."

The rapid decline in the cost of silver, which was largely due to a shift in government policy and a margin call that the Hunts couldn't cover, wiped out much of silver's inflated value, affecting not just William and Nelson Hunt but also a great number of bullion speculators and coin dealers who had untold sums of money tied up in price-inflated silver. The crash also soured investors on gold, which spent much of the next decade as a low-growth commodity.

When the dust settled, the GSA resumed its plan to sell its remaining Morgan dollars. In July 1980 the last of the government's Uncirculated 1880-CCs were offered for $180 per coin. The 4,281 coins sold out almost immediately.

Uncirculated 1880-CCs tend to grade between MS-62 and MS-65. Higher-end MS-66 pieces exist in sizable numbers, but demand for premium-quality coins keeps them from lingering in the marketplace. Prooflike and deep mirror prooflike coins are available at the similar rate to most early Morgan issues and understandably command significant premiums, especially in DMPL.

1880-CC
Certified Populations and Check List
Mint State

Circ	MS-60	MS-61	MS-62	MS-63	MS-64	MS-65	MS-66	MS-67	MS-68
364	45	244	1,096	3,105	4,432	2,341	717	27	

Prooflike

Circ	MS-60	MS-61	MS-62	MS-63	MS-64	MS-65	MS-66	MS-67	MS-68
	6	22	118	247	275	118	8	1	

Deep Mirror Prooflike

Circ	MS-60	MS-61	MS-62	MS-63	MS-64	MS-65	MS-66	MS-67	MS-68
	1	12	28	77	65	25	2		

1880-O

Mintage 5,305,000

Certified Population. 10,935

Prooflike % 1.93

Deep Mirror Prooflike %. 1.65

In its second year of Morgan dollar production, the New Orleans Mint picked up steam and took some of the pressure off of Philadelphia to produce the legally mandated number of silver dollars. That this was done without modern-day air conditioning during the hot and humid summer months is a testament to the fortitude of the Mint's coining staff, as dehydration was a real and constant threat.

The resulting issue was a mixed bag, literally. While the 1880-O is usually a well-struck coin, it frequently suffers from unsightly bag marks and abrasions. Attractive MS-64 pieces exist that would grade MS-66 without one or two unsightly hits in primary focal areas. As it stands, just 33 examples have graded MS-65, and it's a big event whenever one goes on sale.

Another thing to keep in mind is that the 1880-O is an issue with a lot of About Uncirculated sliders. The New Orleans Mint did a great job distributing their coins, but the unwieldy silver dollars found their way back to the Treasury with minimal use. Numerous mint-sewn bags filled with AU coins have turned up over the years, which make Uncirculated coins premium in the MS-62 through MS-64 range.

Prooflike and deep mirror prooflike coins are exceptionally rare for this issue. PCGS has graded fewer than 400, with typical coins grading between MS-60 and MS-64. The issue also has a number of overdates and "O" mintmark varieties.

1880-O
Certified Populations and Check List
Mint State

Circ	MS-60	MS-61	MS-62	MS-63	MS-64	MS-65	MS-66	MS-67	MS-68
3,017	244	1,015	2,576	2,383	1,296	33			

Prooflike

Circ	MS-60	MS-61	MS-62	MS-63	MS-64	MS-65	MS-66	MS-67	MS-68
	28	46	68	45	23	1			

Deep Mirror Prooflike

Circ	MS-60	MS-61	MS-62	MS-63	MS-64	MS-65	MS-66	MS-67	MS-68
	23	27	44	46	40	1			

1880-S

Mintage 8,900,000

Certified Population......... 145,945

Prooflike % 7.77

Deep Mirror Prooflike %..... 1.82

For the second straight year, the San Francisco Mint produced one silver coin denomination—the Morgan dollar. Production in 1880 dropped by a negligible 210,000 coins compared to the year before, and the San Francisco Mint was again second in total dollar production behind Philadelphia. Unlike Morgan dollars struck elsewhere this year, the 1880-S Morgan stuns with its consistently high quality.

That "high quality" wasn't always appreciated, however, as David Hendrickson of SilverTowne explains: "Back in 1962 to 1964, my dad (Leon Hendrickson) and I would fly to Washington, D.C., four times a week to buy bags at face value from the Treasury Department. You couldn't look inside the bags or choose the bags you want. You got what they gave you. My dad and I could carry four bags apiece, so he, I, and another person would buy 12 bags and haul them out of the vaults by hand and take them back to Winchester, Indiana, by airplane. When we got home, we'd open the bags and if it was an 1879-S, 1880-S, or 1881-S bag, it was the pits!"

Amazingly, in 1962, no special attention was paid to the quality of the coin. Collectors of the period believed that Uncirculated coins had to come blast white, and no one paid any attention to whether coins had frost on the devices or not. In the 1960s, margins for common-date Morgans were so slim that it made more sense to take the coins back to the bank and deposit them at a loss (banks would charge handling fees on bulk dollar deposits) than to try to sell them. When silver had its unprecedented run-up in the late 1970s untold hundreds if not thousands of brilliant Uncirculated original bags of this date were emptied into the smelter's furnace, by some accounts.

Today, the 1880-S and its common-date San Francisco counterparts of other years get the respect they deserve and rank among the most attractive dollar coins ever struck. The numismatic value of the Morgan dollar far exceeds the coin's intrinsic worth, and original Uncirculated bags have become scarce.

The typical 1880-S in Uncirculated condition grades MS-63 to MS-65. Superior examples in MS-66 and above are available. This is one of the more common dates to find prooflike coins and deep mirror prooflike.

1880-S
Certified Populations and Check List
Mint State

Circ	MS-60	MS-61	MS-62	MS-63	MS-64	MS-65	MS-66	MS-67	MS-68
367	115	756	4,813	28,226	53,179	32,846	9,625	1,853	172

Prooflike

Circ	MS-60	MS-61	MS-62	MS-63	MS-64	MS-65	MS-66	MS-67	MS-68
	20	142	700	2,936	4,233	2,499	672	114	17

Deep Mirror Prooflike

Circ	MS-60	MS-61	MS-62	MS-63	MS-64	MS-65	MS-66	MS-67	MS-68
	8	25	204	672	926	610	186	27	2

1881

Mintage 9,163,000
Certified Population. 11,545
Prooflike % 2.45
Deep Mirror Prooflike %. 1.49

For the first time in the Morgan dollar's short production life, the Philadelphia Mint wasn't carrying the burden of minting the most coins for the year; that responsibility fell to San Francisco.

By 1881 the mints of the United States were organizationally structured in such a fashion that Philadelphia would fulfill a majority of America's coining needs (the mint handled all cent production and the production of nearly all minor coinage) and San Francisco would serve all of California and some locations to the east of the Rockies.

In theory, Carson City would assist San Francisco and proliferate its coins in the Western frontier states—this of course was contingent on the Nevada mint getting sufficient bullion for coining. In the East, the New Orleans Mint's role would be to strike coins for the Southern United States, part of Texas, and the Mississippi River region. In practice, New Orleans mostly assisted Philadelphia in fulfilling its legal responsibilities in striking Morgan dollars.

While the Silverites had fed the populace an idea where silver dollars would flow into the hands of the workers, increasing America's money supply, the reality of the situation was dollars were being stacked from floor to ceiling in Mint facilities and many of the dollars that were distributed were being returned by the banks.

Those in favor of silver didn't have much of an ally in the newly elected president. James A. Garfield, a moderate Republican from Ohio, supported a gold standard, and had worked closely with his late friend, former Treasury secretary and chief justice Salmon P. Chase, on a number of economic issues.

Tragically, Garfield's term in office was cut short after he was shot by the itinerant preacher and Stalwart (Republican faction) supporter Charles Guiteau. Garfield lingered in bed for eight agonizing weeks after the shooting, and quite possibly would have survived if not for the infighting and alleged incompetence of his team of doctors.

When Stalwart Republican and Garfield's vice president, Chester Alan Arthur, became president upon Garfield's death, he too was outspoken in his belief that the Bland-Allison Act was a failure. This brought to three the number of chief executives who did not support the production of the silver dollar. Arthur repeated his opposition to the coin in the 1884 campaign.

Returning to the Morgan dollar: In terms of a quality, the 1881 Philly strike is generally passable. Coins tend to have an average or better strike, unless the example was struck using an overused die. Bag marks are the norm, but the issue isn't one of the baggier dates. The average Uncirculated grade for the issue is from MS-62 to MS-64. Prooflike and deep mirror prooflike coins are scarce.

1881
Certified Populations and Check List
Mint State

Circ	MS-60	MS-61	MS-62	MS-63	MS-64	MS-65	MS-66	MS-67	MS-68
267	33	150	1,231	4,319	4,043	960	85	2	

Prooflike

Circ	MS-60	MS-61	MS-62	MS-63	MS-64	MS-65	MS-66	MS-67	MS-68
	14	21	64	107	65	12			

Deep Mirror Prooflike

Circ	MS-60	MS-61	MS-62	MS-63	MS-64	MS-65	MS-66	MS-67	MS-68
	6	19	38	40	62	7			

1881-CC

Mintage 296,000

Certified Population. 20,974

Prooflike % 4.99

Deep Mirror Prooflike %. 5.46

If the Carson City Mint was thought of as the San Francisco Mint's underachieving little sister, then 1881 must have been a disaster, as coining operations were suspended for six out of twelve months, in part due to a scandal where mint workers were accused of "sweating" gold ingots, a practice where gold dust is collected from ingots which are purposefully abused. The total output in coins for 1881: 24,015 eagles, a paltry 13,886 half eagles, and a mere 296,000 Morgan dollars.

Estimates vary as to how many 1881-CC dollars originally made it into circulation. The coin was considered scarce through the mid-1950s, when Uncirculated examples traded for $470 in inflation-adjusted dollars. A notable release of bags from the Treasury wiped out much of the coins' value, which steadily climbed again before the public announcement that nearly half of the issue was to be offered in the GSA sales of the 1970s.

This news unnerved many dealers and investors, who warned their clients that the coin was overvalued with so many examples getting ready to be dumped on the market. However, these fears, though based in logic, turned out to be, in part, unfounded. The GSA hoard did contain half of the issue's coins in brilliant Uncirculated condition, but there were more than enough interested parties willing to pay what could best be described as a high retail price for them.

If you are comparing today's prices for the 1881-CC against the coin's 1950 value, you will see a flat line (with the exception of coins in the upper Mint State register). Considering what collectors and dealers now know about the population of Mint State survivors, the coin has actually performed very well and should continue to do so.

In terms of quality, the 1881-CC comes one to one and a half points better in Uncirculated condition than CC-Mint dollars from previous years. Prooflike and deep mirror prooflike coins are obtainable for those wishing to collect them.

1881-CC
Certified Populations and Check List
Mint State

Circ	MS-60	MS-61	MS-62	MS-63	MS-64	MS-65	MS-66	MS-67	MS-68
328	29	176	1,160	4,148	7,073	4,301	1,421	142	3

Prooflike

Circ	MS-60	MS-61	MS-62	MS-63	MS-64	MS-65	MS-66	MS-67	MS-68
	8	24	106	332	390	157	30		

Deep Mirror Prooflike

Circ	MS-60	MS-61	MS-62	MS-63	MS-64	MS-65	MS-66	MS-67	MS-68
	12	12	104	319	446	203	50	1	

1881-O

Mintage 5,708,000

Certified Population. 16,501

Prooflike % 3.48

Deep Mirror Prooflike %. 6.19

In 1881 the Treasury Department continued to use the New Orleans branch's additional capacity to produce Morgan dollars. Except for the production of 8,350 eagles, this was the facility's sole task.

Mint Director Horatio Burchard said in his annual report that demand for the coin was strong, with more than six million dollars distributed over the course of the year.[8] The evidence of distribution is seen in the large amount of barely circulated examples, which coin dealer Dean Tavenner called "two-beer" dollars. Tavenner and subsequent numismatists have never quite figured out why so many coins circulated for such a brief period of time. Some of these barely used pieces even wound up back in

Mint bags, according to Q. David Bowers, who wrote in depth about the topic in his *Encyclopedia*.

The existence of so many briefly circulated coins in the marketplace is a great reason to choose a certified example. The number of certified circulated examples of common-date New Orleans Morgan dollars attests to the difficulty of telling them apart from Uncirculated coins.

The 1881-O is one of the better-date coins from this branch mint. Strike ranges from average to a little bit above. Due to the prevalence of bag marks, the typical grade of the issue remains below gem. Expect most Uncirculated examples to grade from MS-62 to MS-64. The same holds true for prooflike coins, which are actually a grade worse on the high side. For whatever reason, deep mirror prooflikes are clustered between MS-63 and MS-64.

1881-O
Certified Populations and Check List
Mint State

Circ	MS-60	MS-61	MS-62	MS-63	MS-64	MS-65	MS-66	MS-67	MS-68
1,134	142	634	2,914	6,116	3,388	561	15		

Prooflike

Circ	MS-60	MS-61	MS-62	MS-63	MS-64	MS-65	MS-66	MS-67	MS-68
	13	77	203	192	86	4			

Deep Mirror Prooflike

Circ	MS-60	MS-61	MS-62	MS-63	MS-64	MS-65	MS-66	MS-67	MS-68
	24	55	149	358	424	12			

1881-S

Mintage 12,760,000

Certified Population. 234,487

Prooflike % 3.73

Deep Mirror Prooflike % 0.44

As mentioned earlier, 1881 marks the apex of Morgan dollar production out of San Francisco, and this issue was the first of two instances when the West Coast mint out-produced Philadelphia. In Philadelphia's defense, they did strike more than 50 million coins this year, including 9,586,062 gold eagles and half eagles.

The impetus for this massive production was statutory and not directly related to public demand for the coin, as later releases of Mint bags indicate that the 1881-S did not circulate in any significant way at the time of production. Readily available stockpiles of Mint State coins clogged up private bank and Treasury Department vaults through the early 1960s. A phenomenon called Gresham's Law, which holds that bad money chases out good money, made 90 percent silver coins, especially silver dollar coins, attractive, and the once-unwelcome coins became an investment vehicle for anyone who could afford to buy and hold onto them.

As a numismatic item, the 1881-S remained a common-date coin well through the end of the 1960s, one that scarcely generated more than 1.5 times or double face value through the end of the 1960s. John Love recounts seeing hundreds of bags of 1881-S dollars in the Redfield and Continental-Illinois Bank hoards, which were dispersed in the 1970s and 1980s.

As silver approached its peak in the late 1970s, untold tens of thousands of 1881-S and other common issues were indiscriminately melted, some have suggested. Whether these bags contained beautiful high-end pieces we'll never know. And as there was no proper accounting of what was being destroyed, we may never know how many 1881-S dollars survive.

Today, the 1881-S is a type-set coin. Abundant in Mint State, it continues the streak of great-looking San Francisco Morgan dollars. The typical Uncirculated 1881-S dollar grades between MS-63 and MS-65. More than 12,000 examples have been certified MS-66, and for those looking for the ultimate in quality, nearly 100 examples have graded MS-68. The issue is readily available in prooflike, but scarce in deep mirror prooflike.

1881-S
Certified Populations and Check List
Mint State

Circ	MS-60	MS-61	MS-62	MS-63	MS-64	MS-65	MS-66	MS-67	MS-68
558	203	1,645	10,817	58,178	91,480	47,902	12,176	1,653	99

Prooflike

Circ	MS-60	MS-61	MS-62	MS-63	MS-64	MS-65	MS-66	MS-67	MS-68
	17	71	496	2,407	3,322	1,874	485	67	2

Deep Mirror Prooflike

Circ	MS-60	MS-61	MS-62	MS-63	MS-64	MS-65	MS-66	MS-67	MS-68
	6	15	65	302	344	225	71	6	1

1882

Mintage	11,100,00
Certified Population	15,217
Prooflike %	2.07
Deep Mirror Prooflike %	1.68

While American economic power continued to consolidate under the yoke of the robber barons, the mints of the United States continued to faithfully discharge their duty in producing the requisite number of Morgan dollars, with the Philadelphia Mint leading the charge.

In 1882, Philadelphia's total output approached 55 million coins, about 150,000 a day. The majority of these were the economic heavy lifters: Indian Head cents and Shield nickels. Morgan dollar production accounted for 11,100,000 of the overall total. Not every denomination saw mass production, however; coinage of quarters and half dollars continued its prolonged slump and the anemic production of double eagles created one of the series' great rarities. Gold dollars, quarter eagles, and

three-dollar pieces were also struck in limited quantities, as was the nickel three-cent piece.

The quality of 1882 P-Mint Morgan dollars varies from very nice to weak. The key factors for determining the quality of the piece are die state and the quality of the coin's surfaces. The average Uncirculated examples tend to cluster in the MS-63 to MS-64 range. Gem-quality pieces are readily available for a premium.

Prooflike and deep mirror prooflike examples from this issue are scarce, which is characteristic for Philadelphia-minted dollars, as the Mint was more concerned about producing coins on a massive scale (by getting the most out of their dies) than on eye appeal. With more than 15,000 coins certified by PCGS, the total number of prooflike and deep mirror prooflike examples in PCGS holders is below 600, with a majority of these tied up in collections. The coin is particularly underrated in prooflike and DMPL MS-64.

1882
Certified Populations and Check List

Mint State

Circ	MS-60	MS-61	MS-62	MS-63	MS-64	MS-65	MS-66	MS-67	MS-68
309	47	214	1,714	6,002	4,887	1,262	206	6	

Prooflike

Circ	MS-60	MS-61	MS-62	MS-63	MS-64	MS-65	MS-66	MS-67	MS-68
	2	14	53	123	96	26	1		

Deep Mirror Prooflike

Circ	MS-60	MS-61	MS-62	MS-63	MS-64	MS-65	MS-66	MS-67	MS-68
	3	14	41	84	91	21	1		

1882-CC

Mintage 1,133,000

Certified Population. 32,324

Prooflike % 6.96

Deep Mirror Prooflike %. 6.43

In 1882, the Carson City Mint continued to produce small quantities of Morgan dollars, most of which were stored in government vaults and never released for circulation. Bags of 1882-CC dollars trickled out on occasion, but most of the mintage remained warehoused until the early 1960s.

Pricing for the 1882-CC has been erratic over the years. Values fluctuated throughout the first half of the century until the pressures of increased demand sent the cost of Uncirculated examples northward of $35 in 1972. When the General Services Administration announced that they held just over 605,000 pieces, of which 382,913 were deemed "Uncirculated" by GSA inspectors[9], there were more than a few naysayers in the industry. You could hardly blame collectors and dealers for being leery. This total represented more than half of the coin's total mintage. If there weren't a number of collectors clamoring for the coin in excess of what was now known to be available, prices could plummet.

It turned out, however, that they were wrong. The GSA sales brought many new buy-ers into the market and raised the public's awareness of the series. So, while some, like the *Coin Dealer Newsletter's* Allen Harriman, warned that the value of the 1882-CC and some of the other CC Mint issues would fall to about $3 to $5, the reality was that the coin maintained almost all of its premium despite the fact that it took the government three different sales to finally sell out of it.

Today, 1882-CC dollars in GSA holders are actually more coveted than the coins by themselves! And while the population figures listed below primarily account for coins that have been cracked out of GSA packaging and placed in PCGS holders, PCGS has now developed a certification option for those wishing to get the coin accurately graded without removing the coin from the GSA casing.

In terms of preservation, the 1882-CC is a quality issue, with many coins grading MS-64 and MS-65. Most coins have attractive eye appeal and are well struck. Beautiful toners exist also, and many of these were sold at a reduced price in the GSA Mixed CC sales, since the inspectors were not trained to differentiate attractive natural toning from wear.

For those looking for prooflike and deep mirror prooflike coins, the 1882-CC offers a robust population at only a modest premium.

1882-CC
Certified Populations and Check List
Mint State

Circ	MS-60	MS-61	MS-62	MS-63	MS-64	MS-65	MS-66	MS-67	MS-68
427	67	408	2,340	7,896	10,711	4,912	1,175	61	1

Prooflike

Circ	MS-60	MS-61	MS-62	MS-63	MS-64	MS-65	MS-66	MS-67	MS-68
	3	25	220	732	832	359	77	1	

Deep Mirror Prooflike

Circ	MS-60	MS-61	MS-62	MS-63	MS-64	MS-65	MS-66	MS-67	MS-68
	7	32	234	577	810	354	62	1	

1882-O

Mintage 6,090,000

Certified Population. 19,029

Prooflike % 3.24

Deep Mirror Prooflike %. 2.69

The New Orleans Mint continued to deliver dollars at a respectable rate, coining 6,090,000 in 1882. Stockpiles of non-circulating dollars in San Francisco forced the Philadelphia Mint to shift production to New Orleans. This would become more apparent in 1883 and beyond, but we see in the 1882-O a continued reliance on New Orleans to carry out the statutory directive of the Bland-Allison Act.

That the Morgan dollar scarcely circulated in any of the regions where it was struck spoke to the flaw behind the act, which was the assumption that Americans wanted to carry the heavy coins. Frustration over this issue would continue to build on both sides of the partisan divide.

Today, the 1882-O in Mint State is a common issue, but in grades above MS-65 it's conditionally scarce. In the days before third-party grading, one had to know the series fairly well to avoid paying Uncirculated prices for barely circulated coins, as a sealed Mint bag was no indicator of the virgin nature of its contents. To make matters worse, the typical example is softly struck and many have subdued toning, especially if it was stored in a roll for long periods of time. Thankfully, contemporary collectors have the benefit of coin certification to alleviate concerns that they might get stuck with almost barely circulated coins, commonly referred to as *sliders*.

The 1882-O, like the 1882, is scarce in prooflike and deep mirror prooflike. Most examples grade from MS-62 to MS-64. Gems are rarely encountered. Another interesting opportunity exists with this date, and that's the 1882-O, O Over S overmintmark. This variety is available in sufficient enough quantities that you might even find one *un*attributed in a third-party-graded holder. The typical grade for it is consistent with the issue overall, but only two examples are known in MS-65. The last one of those to sell at auction fetched over $42,000!

1882-O
Certified Populations and Check List
Mint State

Circ	MS-60	MS-61	MS-62	MS-63	MS-64	MS-65	MS-66	MS-67	MS-68
922	121	539	2,800	7,568	5,184	741	22	3	1

Prooflike

Circ	MS-60	MS-61	MS-62	MS-63	MS-64	MS-65	MS-66	MS-67	MS-68
	12	37	139	234	158	36	1		

Deep Mirror Prooflike

Circ	MS-60	MS-61	MS-62	MS-63	MS-64	MS-65	MS-66	MS-67	MS-68
	10	34	120	188	138	20	1		

1882-S

Mintage 9,250,000

Certified Population. 74,105

Prooflike % 2.99

Deep Mirror Prooflike %. 0.27

By June of 1882, the San Francisco Mint was teeming with unwanted Morgan dollars. Mint Director Horatio Burchard in his annual report noted that more than 25 million coins (a little more than 81 percent of the total S-Mint output from 1879 to 1881) were being stored in the San Francisco vault, while only 1.8 million coins were distributed during the prior year. Since the coins were being struck not for demand, but simply to comply with the Bland-Allison Act, there was nothing the Mint could do but continue to stockpile dollar coins.

To put the vast quantity of San Francisco's stored dollar coins in perspective, 25 million coins equals 25,000 $1,000 bags, which have a combined weight of 1.5 million pounds!

The 1882-S is like most early San Francisco issues and is typically found in premium grades, MS-63 through MS-65. PCGS has certified a few thousand examples in MS-66, which sell for about double the cost of a gem. Prooflike for this date are on the scarce side, while deep mirror prooflike coins are rarely encountered.

Miles remembers: "I'd like to add a personal experience of mine about the 1882-S dollar. In the winter of 1984, my dad and I drove for several hours through snow from Kalamazoo, Michigan, to Dave and Leon Hendrickson's Winchester, Indiana, cathedral of coins, Silver-Towne. Dave and Leon had just gotten their hands on a large swath of the Continental-Illinois Bank hoard. When we arrived, Leon Hendrickson greeted us and took us back to his personal office, where he asked me to take a seat at his desk. At 19 years old, sitting at Leon's desk at the center of the coin universe in front of my dad was a moment I'll never forget.

"Leon put me in charge and rolled over a cart with bags of 1882-S dollars from the Continental-Illinois Bank hoard and roll after roll of fresh BU Morgan dollars. I was on the edge of my seat at getting this opportunity to 'pick' such a historic deal. My dad and I worked all day and into the night, sorting through coins and picking the best. At the end of the day, Leon and his son David loaded our car up and we made our way home through the winter wonderland of Indiana and back to Kalamazoo."

1882-S
Certified Populations and Check List
Mint State

Circ	MS-60	MS-61	MS-62	MS-63	MS-64	MS-65	MS-66	MS-67	MS-68
211	55	279	2,787	17,006	29,303	16,789	4,469	749	43

Prooflike

Circ	MS-60	MS-61	MS-62	MS-63	MS-64	MS-65	MS-66	MS-67	MS-68
	6	32	130	638	905	423	76	4	

Deep Mirror Prooflike

Circ	MS-60	MS-61	MS-62	MS-63	MS-64	MS-65	MS-66	MS-67	MS-68
		4	17	64	73	34	8		

1883

Mintage 12,290,000
Certified Population. 22,260
Prooflike % 2.58
Deep Mirror Prooflike %. 3.17

Already drowning in a sea of unwanted silver coins, Mint Director Horatio C. Burchard pleaded with Congress to reconsider the Bland-Allison Act in the 1883 *Annual Report of the Director of the Mint,* citing a stockpile of more than a hundred million dollars' worth of excess coins. The continued attempt to impose a bimetallic standard without "the co-operation of leading commercial nations" was clearly not working.[10]

The best evidence came from the Mint's distribution record, which showed that the San Francisco Mint had distributed only 1.6 million coins as of June 30, while maintaining a stockpile of almost 31 million. In order to comply with Bland-Allison, the director had to shift production emphasis from San Francisco to New Orleans. There was no point in increasing production at Carson City.

In 1883, the Philadelphia Mint continued to carry most of the coining responsibilities for the country. In total, the Mother Mint struck 12,290,000 Morgan dollars. A majority of the coins struck are of high quality with exceptional luster. The typical PCGS certified grade for the issue falls between MS-63 and MS-65.

Physical contact with other coins makes superb gems elusive, but it's almost impossible to expect otherwise when you're moving 57-pound bags around and piling them ceiling-high on top of one another. This is how they were stored until the Mint liquidated its stock in the 1960s.

More deep mirror prooflike examples have been certified by PCGS than prooflikes—an uncommon occurrence in the series that is more likely the result of sample size than an indication of the quality of the general population. Because of this, we see a slight devaluation of prooflike issues. Taken as a whole, however, 1883 is an underrated issue for PLs and DMPLs.

What a Racket: In 1883, the Liberty Head nickel, commonly referred to as the "V" nickel, debuted. Charles Barber's design emulated the Morgan dollar's interpretation of Miss Liberty and featured the Roman numeral V instead of the Arabic numeral 5 that appeared on the Shield nickel (1861–1883). The new nickel also omitted the words CENTS, which led some enterprising con artists to gold-plate the coin and pass it off as a five-dollar gold piece. Complaints poured in and the Mint quickly revised the design.

1883
Certified Populations and Check List
Mint State

Circ	MS-60	MS-61	MS-62	MS-63	MS-64	MS-65	MS-66	MS-67	MS-68
290	21	150	1,282	6,145	8,279	3,869	853	89	1

Prooflike

Circ	MS-60	MS-61	MS-62	MS-63	MS-64	MS-65	MS-66	MS-67	MS-68
	8	16	75	223	193	57	3		

Deep Mirror Prooflike

Circ	MS-60	MS-61	MS-62	MS-63	MS-64	MS-65	MS-66	MS-67	MS-68
	5	23	110	232	244	83	9		

1883-CC

Mintage	1,204,000
Certified Population.	43,648
Prooflike %	7.67
Deep Mirror Prooflike %.	8.01

In 1883 the Carson City Mint worked year round, producing Morgan dollars and gold coins in denominations of $5 and up. The monetary value of all coins struck by the Carson City Mint increased slightly from 1882 to 1883, helped in large part by the mint's output of 12,000 eagles and 59,962 double eagles. Production of Morgan dollars ticked up slightly, with the yearly total reaching 1,204,000 coins. Still, most of the mint's output of silver dollars did not circulate, unlike the $5 and $10 Liberty Head gold coins, which have only a few known examples of each in Mint State.

First offered for $30 ($162 in today's dollars[11]) in the October 1972 to March 1973 GSA sale, the 1883-CC was the second-most abundant Carson City issue in the federal govern-

ment's holdings. It went on sale again at the same price in June and July of 1973, and then for $60 ($164) in February 1980. Of the 1.2 million coins struck, only a third were ever released into circulation, and most of those, according to anecdotal evidence, were released in the 20th century.

Today the coin is reasonably well dispersed (this hasn't always been the case) and all but the occasional low-end example have appreciated in value well beyond the government's asking price. The average certified grade for the issue is between MS-63 and MS-65, with more than 2,000 examples judged by PCGS to be MS-66 or better.

The 1883-CC features some of the nicest prooflike and deep mirror prooflike coins in the entire series. The prevalence of PL and DMPL coins is the result of high-quality coin production and the large percentage of Uncirculated coins sold to the public in GSA cases.

1883-CC
Certified Populations and Check List
Mint State

Circ	MS-60	MS-61	MS-62	MS-63	MS-64	MS-65	MS-66	MS-67	MS-68
344	96	442	2,726	9,414	14,208	7,568	1,841	153	5

Prooflike

Circ	MS-60	MS-61	MS-62	MS-63	MS-64	MS-65	MS-66	MS-67	MS-68
	6	42	331	1,012	1,220	590	144	8	

Deep Mirror Prooflike

Circ	MS-60	MS-61	MS-62	MS-63	MS-64	MS-65	MS-66	MS-67	MS-68
	8	43	280	987	1,326	735	117	2	

1883-O

Mintage 8,725,000

Certified Population 105,678

Prooflike % 2.18

Deep Mirror Prooflike % 1.53

A spike in production at New Orleans corresponded to a decrease in San Francisco's output. Government vaults on the West Coast were filling up, so in order to comply with Bland-Allison, the director of the Mint shifted resources to the Southeast. In total, the New Orleans Mint produced 8,725,000 silver dollars over the course of the year. Considering that only a fraction of them actually circulated, the only thing keeping the last Southern branch mint in business was an ill-advised act of Congress.

Horatio C. Burchard, who before his appointment by President Rutherford B. Hayes to the position of Mint director sat on the powerful House Ways and Means Committee, put it bluntly when he said of the branch mint, "this institution is of little local advantage."[12]

The 1883-O has long been considered one of the most readily available Morgan dollar issues. Millions were dispersed during the 1960s, and David Hendrickson of SilverTowne recalls seeing thousands of pieces in the famous Continental-Illinois Bank hoard.

Strike quality for the 1883-O varies wildly. Much of this has to do with the condition of the dies, which New Orleans' coiners liked to push to the limit. PCGS has certified more than 100,000 pieces from this issue, with the majority of the Uncirculated examples grading between MS-62 and MS-65. Prooflike and deep mirror prooflike coins are available in sufficient quantity for the marketplace, but are by percentage less common than most dates.

1883-O
Certified Populations and Check List
Mint State

Circ	MS-60	MS-61	MS-62	MS-63	MS-64	MS-65	MS-66	MS-67	MS-68
438	270	1,667	11,528	43,780	35,989	7,337	712	37	

Prooflike

Circ	MS-60	MS-61	MS-62	MS-63	MS-64	MS-65	MS-66	MS-67	MS-68
	50	152	469	874	596	153	13		

Deep Mirror Prooflike

Circ	MS-60	MS-61	MS-62	MS-63	MS-64	MS-65	MS-66	MS-67	MS-68
	26	75	326	582	493	96	15		

Mintage 6,250,000

Certified Population. 5,451

Prooflike % 0.40

Deep Mirror Prooflike %. 0.04

For the third year in a row, the San Francisco Mint lowered its production of Morgan dollars by roughly a third. The 6,250,000 pieces struck in California was less than the total struck by both Philadelphia and New Orleans. This marks the first time in the series that output of S-Mint dollars fell below any other branch mint.

That more than six million coins were struck in San Francisco in 1883 is irrelevant to the position the coin has always held in the marketplace, as the 1883-S is the first of the scarce S-Mint issues. The Treasury dispersed no bags of 1883-S Morgans in the 1960s, and the coins, while in regular supply in the 1950s, were well distributed by the time the market for Morgan dollars really started to heat up in the mid- to late 1960s.

In the 1970s collectors got one more crack at a large grouping of 1883-S dollars, as the Redfield hoard contained a few hundred examples. These coins quickly sold out.

The 1960 *Red Book* listed the coin at $5 ($38.23, adjusted for inflation) in brilliant Uncirculated and $1.50 in Extremely Fine.[13] The January 20, 1965, *Coin Dealer Newsletter* had no bid on the coin but it did have an asking price of $20 ($143) for Uncirculated singles. By the middle of the 1970s, the price had ballooned to $275 ($1,401), and once numerical grading was instituted, premiums for higher-end examples grew significantly.

By current grading standards, we now know that the coin is rare in gem, with fewer than 20 graded as such by PCGS. The average certified Uncirculated piece falls between MS-61 and MS-64, with most being choice. The days of cheap Uncs being sold by the roll are long since over and even barely circulated AU coins bring strong money.

The 1883-S is one of the toughest dates for prooflike or deep mirror prooflike examples. Few are known, and the issue is rarely available at coin shows. To date PCGS has designated exactly 2 as DMPL, while 22 coins, including a superb gem once owned by renowned collectors J.M. Clapp and Louis E. Eliasberg, are designated prooflike.

1883-S
Certified Populations and Check List
Mint State

Circ	MS-60	MS-61	MS-62	MS-63	MS-64	MS-65	MS-66	MS-67	MS-68
2,761	143	409	819	871	407	14	2	1	

Prooflike

Circ	MS-60	MS-61	MS-62	MS-63	MS-64	MS-65	MS-66	MS-67	MS-68
	1	7	4	7	1		1	1	

Deep Mirror Prooflike

Circ	MS-60	MS-61	MS-62	MS-63	MS-64	MS-65	MS-66	MS-67	MS-68
		1			1				

1884

Mintage 14,070,000

Certified Population 15,108

Prooflike % 2.45

Deep Mirror Prooflike % 1.85

The mints of the United States continued to juggle resources in order to meet the demands of the Bland-Allison Act. The San Francisco vaults were overburdened with undistributed coins, which continued to force the Mint to shift the bulk of the coin's production to Philadelphia and New Orleans. In 1884, both of these mints outproduced their 1883 totals. For the fourth year in a row, San Francisco's output was significantly less than the year before, this time by about 50 percent. The Philadelphia Mint shouldered most of the burden, turning out most of the nation's circulating coinage alongside a total of 14,070,000 Morgan dollars.

Congress deliberated over the possibility of opening a new branch mint in St. Louis, Missouri, to better serve the Midwestern states. A report issued by the Honorable Richard "Silver Dick" Bland endorsed this proposal, citing savings in transportation costs, among other things. And while the report showed that little more than a quarter of the Morgan dollars struck

since 1878 had been released into circulation (with that number in severe decline since 1881), no serious consideration was given on the part of the silver proponents to curb coin production or even repeal the failure that was the Bland-Allison Act.

For what it's worth, a fair number of 1884 Philly-strike Morgan dollars did circulate as intended—not nearly enough to turn this coin into a scarce date, however, so a number of bags remained unopened well into the 1970s. As SilverTowne's David Hendrickson relates, their portion of the Continental-Illinois Bank hoard contained at least a dozen brilliant Uncirculated unopened Mint bags of them.[14]

Typical quality for this issue is good, with solid strikes and ample luster. Expect bag marks, unfortunately, as they are the norm. Also, keep a lookout for a number of interesting varieties, such as the enigmatic VAM 3 and the VAM 4, which features small dots next to the designer's initial on the obverse and reverse.

Despite the easy availability of bags through the first three quarters of the 20th century, the 1884 Philly strike yielded but precious few prooflike and deep mirror prooflike coins. Nevertheless, prices are modest up to MS-64 for PL and MS-63 for DMPL.

1884
Certified Populations and Check List
Mint State

Circ	MS-60	MS-61	MS-62	MS-63	MS-64	MS-65	MS-66	MS-67	MS-68
420	21	177	1,226	4,622	5,450	2,078	426	36	2

Prooflike

Circ	MS-60	MS-61	MS-62	MS-63	MS-64	MS-65	MS-66	MS-67	MS-68
	6	17	64	136	118	24	4	1	

Deep Mirror Prooflike

Circ	MS-60	MS-61	MS-62	MS-63	MS-64	MS-65	MS-66	MS-67	MS-68
	1	10	50	81	101	32	5		

1884-CC

Mintage	1,136,000
Certified Population.	46,642
Prooflike %	6.67
Deep Mirror Prooflike %.	6.98

In 1884 the mint at Carson City produced 9,925 eagles and 81,139 double eagles. Both of these issues circulated freely, leaving modern collectors with precious few examples in Mint State   especially in the case of the eagle. The mint also produced 1,136,000 Morgan dollars, a total only slightly off from the year before. Nearly all of this issue went from press to storage.

Rarely encountered in circulation, the coin eluded many early Morgan dollar collectors before a few bags of Uncirculated coins trickled out in the 1950s. Enough 1884-CC dollars were released that the issue was trading for $4 ($30 adjusted for inflation) by 1960. After the Treasury stopped releasing Morgan dollars at face value in 1964, that price shot up, and by 1967 the issue had a bid/ask of $22.50/$24 ($152/$162).[15] By the time the GSA revealed that it held 962,638 pieces (788,630 of which qualified as Uncirculated), it had become apparent where the majority of the mintage had been hiding.

As was the case with the 1883-CC, the GSA offered Uncirculated examples in four separate offerings. At a $30 minimum bid ($162), the coin was offered in the sales of October 1972 to March 1973, June to July 1973, and April to June 1974. At a $65 minimum bid ($178), the coin was offered in the penultimate GSA sale held in February 1980, where more than 428,000 pieces were sold.

The glut of inventory on the market worried some dealers, who compared the 1884-CC to the common 1921-P. This turned out to be wrong due to the public way in which the Carson City coins were sold; this invited untold thousands of Americans into the hobby. The perception of value and the cultural resonance of the coins as a relic of the Old West not only allowed the coins to hold their pre-hoard value, but also made the issue a perennial favorite for Morgan dollar enthusiasts.

The mean grade of an 1884-CC, according to PCGS, falls between MS-63 and MS-64.[16] Gems are available in sufficient quantities, and the coin doesn't become conditionally rare until MS-67. For those who like frosted cameos, there are ample numbers of prooflike and deep mirror prooflike coins, with prooflikes commanding just a slight premium over the typical Uncirculated coin of the same grade.

1884-CC
Certified Populations and Check List

Mint State

Circ	MS-60	MS-61	MS-62	MS-63	MS-64	MS-65	MS-66	MS-67	MS-68
135	105	594	3,710	11,617	15,457	7,109	1,471	74	3

Prooflike

Circ	MS-60	MS-61	MS-62	MS-63	MS-64	MS-65	MS-66	MS-67	MS-68
	9	39	290	943	1,269	471	88	1	

Deep Mirror Prooflike

Circ	MS-60	MS-61	MS-62	MS-63	MS-64	MS-65	MS-66	MS-67	MS-68
	11	43	261	854	1,381	583	121	3	

1884-O

Mintage 9,730,000

Certified Population......... 171,795

Prooflike % 1.38

Deep Mirror Prooflike %..... 1.22

The decrease in production (read: storage) capacity at the San Francisco Mint shifted the burden back east to the mints at Philadelphia and New Orleans. As mentioned earlier, Mint Director Horatio Burchard saw production capacity of the New Orleans facility as superfluous, since the Treasury was already sitting on a large stockpile of unwanted silver dollars and lower-denomination subsidiary coins. So instead of ordering the facility to strike up circulating denominations in 1884, he employed the branch mint solely for the production of Morgan dollars.

Only about a quarter of the issue likely circulated at all. So, collectors aren't faced with the problem of having tons of sliders complicate their search for a truly Uncirculated piece. In Mint State the 1884-O is plentiful. A majority of the surviving coins from this issue was released in abundance in the early 1960s. Several Mint bags were part of the Continental-Illinois Bank hoard.

The collectability of the issue in Mint State depends on the strike and the number of bag marks. High-quality coins made from fresher dies are available, as are well-struck pieces with an appealing frosty luster. The average Uncirculated grade for the 1884-O is between MS-62 and MS-65.

The issue yields several thousand prooflike and deep mirror prooflike examples, which are nearly evenly split between the two designations. The percentage of these premium coins over the general population is low due only to the large quantities of coins certified by PCGS. If every issue in the series were so represented, you'd find the numbers of 1884-O PL and DMPL coins to be typical of the series.

1884-O
Certified Populations and Check List
Mint State

Circ	MS-60	MS-61	MS-62	MS-63	MS-64	MS-65	MS-66	MS-67	MS-68
360	189	1,257	14,999	71,784	64,261	13,124	1,278	71	1

Prooflike

Circ	MS-60	MS-61	MS-62	MS-63	MS-64	MS-65	MS-66	MS-67	MS-68
	33	98	267	973	756	222	25	1	

Deep Mirror Prooflike

Circ	MS-60	MS-61	MS-62	MS-63	MS-64	MS-65	MS-66	MS-67	MS-68
	22	70	277	710	723	244	49		1

1884-S

Mintage	3,200,000
Certified Population.........	6,235
Prooflike %	0.06
Deep Mirror Prooflike %.....	0.00

With an overabundant supply of undistributed silver dollars under its control, the San Francisco Mint was tasked to produce 3.2 million large cartwheel coins in 1884. This was a nearly 50 percent decrease from the year before. It marked the third straight year of significant declines in Morgan dollar production for the mint, a trend that would continue through 1886. Furthermore, the eastern shift in Morgan dollar production would see San Francisco play only a minor role in the coin's manufacture until the Sherman Act of 1890 compelled the Mint to increase annual production of Morgan dollars.

That the 1884-S turns out to be so rare in Mint State is a bit of a numismatic mystery. Ample evidence exists that the coin did circulate to some degree, as the coin commands only a slight premium up through the About Uncirculated grades. Furthermore, historic pricing indicates that dealers in the first half of the century were unaware of the scarcity of truly Uncirculated coins. The *Red Book* of 1960, for example, lists the price of an Uncirculated 1884-S at $20 (about $150 in today's dollars). In that year 15 issues commanded a higher price, including the 1898, 1902, 1903, and 1904 New Orleans coins, all of which were genuinely scarce at the time, but became common just four years later when the Treasury emptied its cache of Morgan dollars. The 1884-S, however, wasn't a coin that the government had lying around in any kind of quantity.

While there are plenty of circulated 1884-S dollars that survive, there aren't nearly enough of them to lead us to believe that a sizable percentage of this year's issue survived the great dollar melt authorized by the Pittman Act of 1918. San Francisco shipped nearly 100 million surplus dollars to be converted by the British into Indian rupees. Mint records of dates and quantities sold are unavailable, but the answer to the mystery of "Where are the Uncirculated 1884-S dollars?" likely leads to Calcutta.

1884-S
Certified Populations and Check List

Mint State

Circ	MS-60	MS-61	MS-62	MS-63	MS-64	MS-65	MS-66	MS-67	MS-68
5,946	22	101	104	43	12	1		1	1

Prooflike

Circ	MS-60	MS-61	MS-62	MS-63	MS-64	MS-65	MS-66	MS-67	MS-68
	1		2	1					

Deep Mirror Prooflike

Circ	MS-60	MS-61	MS-62	MS-63	MS-64	MS-65	MS-66	MS-67	MS-68

1885

Mintage 17,786,837

Certified Population. 62,084

Prooflike % 2.52

Deep Mirror Prooflike % 2.74

The precipitous decline in the number of Morgan dollars struck in San Francisco and Carson City compelled Philadelphia and New Orleans to make up for the shortfall or risk failing to meet the requirements for coining silver dollars under the Bland-Allison Act. Seven years into production, a lack of storage space for undistributed coins vexed the Mint's senior staff. The San Francisco Mint had no room to store new coins and produced dollars on par with the coin's dispersal. Still, by year's end more than 30 million coins lay in storage on the West Coast.

Carson City, awash with coins and stuck between the mountains and a sparsely populated American Southwest, was shuttered by the end of the year. Outgoing Mint director Horatio Burchard and newly appointed director James P. Kimball utilized New Orleans and Philadelphia to produce the majority of the dollar coins struck in 1885. Taking the lead was the Mother Mint, which produced an unprecedented total of 17,786,837 Morgan dollars.

Today Uncirculated examples of the 1885 are plentiful, and most of them are attractive and well struck. Couple that with the fact that the coin is a large-format silver dollar and nearly 130 years old, and the 1885 Morgan is a perfect introduction to the series.

The coin was widely available in Mint State throughout the 1950s and 1960s. For those seeking quantities from the Treasury Department, the appearance of the 1885 issue in an unmarked bag proved to be an unpleasant sight as those that turned up were often dumped back into circulation at local banks. Almost no regard was paid for preserving the best-quality coins, and because of this MS-66 and better examples are elusive. The typical grade for this issue is similar to the better Philadelphia dates—MS-63 to MS-65.

Roughly 3,000 coins have met PCGS qualifications to earn either prooflike or deep mirror prooflike designations. Most PL and DMPL examples are MS-64 or below.

1885
Certified Populations and Check List

Mint State

Circ	MS-60	MS-61	MS-62	MS-63	MS-64	MS-65	MS-66	MS-67	MS-68
585	62	420	4,423	19,526	24,350	8,043	1,318	94	1

Prooflike

Circ	MS-60	MS-61	MS-62	MS-63	MS-64	MS-65	MS-66	MS-67	MS-68
	10	33	186	504	573	197	57	2	

Deep Mirror Prooflike

Circ	MS-60	MS-61	MS-62	MS-63	MS-64	MS-65	MS-66	MS-67	MS-68
	1	31	179	535	581	300	72	1	

1885-CC

Mintage 228,000

Certified Population. 21,307

Prooflike % 5.36

Deep Mirror Prooflike %. 6.21

The coining presses at the long-maligned Carson City Mint were inoperative at the end of 1885, having struck just 228,000 Morgan dollars and a paltry 9,450 double eagles. In 1886 a majority of the branch mint's on-hand coinage was either put into circulation or shipped to Washington, D.C., or San Francisco. Once considered extremely scarce, the 1885-CC had a turbulent sales record in the first half of the 20th century. In the 1930s, the coin traded for as much as $12.50 apiece, but enough examples trickled out of the Cash Room in Washington, D.C.—and from Mint bags released in Montana—that by 1959 the 1885-CC was being offered in numismatic magazines and coin shops for about $3 each in Uncirculated condition. Yet by 1965, that number had increased to more than $45.

Whatever percentage of the 79,715 coins survived long enough to be distributed to collectors did not satisfy increasing demand, and the coin's low mintage convinced collectors that the issue was scarce. When the GSA announced its holdings in 1972, hearts sank as collectors realized that 65 percent of the total mintage was stacked in 1,000-coin boxes at the U.S. Bullion Depository at West Point (now the West Point Mint). Many believed that the issue was doomed to be common forever, and some dealers advised their clients to avoid the coin altogether.

The naysayers turned out to be all wet. The issue was offered in October 1973 and from April through June of 1974 at a minimum bid of $60. The final 31,564 Uncs were offered at the last GSA sale in July 1980 at a minimum bid of $180. The issue sold out. Even accounting for inflation, the 1885-CC, like all of the Carson City issues, has proven itself a highly desirable numismatic collectible. The lure of the Old West brought in hundreds of thousands of investors, keepsake hunters, and collectors from a wide range of disciplines. And seeing how the 1885-CC is now fairly well dispersed, only a trickle of new material will ever come onto the market. As demand for historical Morgan dollars continues to remain strong, so will the prices for issues once believed common—like the 1885-CC.

The average grade for the 1885-CC is between MS-62 and MS-65, with most certified by PCGS grading MS-64. Prooflike and deep mirror prooflike issues are readily available. Prooflikes carry only a slight premium over brilliants.

1885-CC
Certified Populations and Check List
Mint State

Circ	MS-60	MS-61	MS-62	MS-63	MS-64	MS-65	MS-66	MS-67	MS-68
198	46	249	1,494	4,634	7,174	3,989	1,006	52	1

Prooflike

Circ	MS-60	MS-61	MS-62	MS-63	MS-64	MS-65	MS-66	MS-67	MS-68
	8	35	153	333	420	162	29	1	

Deep Mirror Prooflike

Circ	MS-60	MS-61	MS-62	MS-63	MS-64	MS-65	MS-66	MS-67	MS-68
	9	43	177	391	447	217	37	2	

1885-O

Mintage 9,185,000

Certified Population. 159,243

Prooflike % 1.21

Deep Mirror Prooflike % 1.00

In 1885, the sole purpose of the New Orleans Mint was to produce enough Morgan dollars to help the Philadelphia Mint offset the drop in production from San Francisco and Carson City. The coiners at William Strickland's 50-year-old mint overlooking Esplanade Street acquitted themselves quite well, striking more than nine million dollar coins and nothing else.

While a small percentage of the issue was distributed in the 19th century, the gargantuan mintage served no direct need for circulating coinage, and far more were either melted by authority of the Pittman Act in 1918 or saved in ten-ounce cloth sacks until the government's stockpile of Morgan dollars was exhausted in

the early 1960s. John Love reports that the Treasury released voluminous amounts of 1885-O mint-sewn bags in 1962 and 1963.

Today, the 1885-O is plentiful in certified Uncirculated grades, making the issue an affordable entry point for collectors looking to get into the series. The issue offers collectors a great opportunity to cherrypick for high-quality coins within each grade level, as the quality of strike on the 1885-O varies wildly and is largely dependent on die state. New Orleans continued its tendency of getting the most out of its dies. Many 1885-O's are weakly struck at the coin's center. Numerically, Uncirculated 1885-O's tend to grade between MS-63 and MS-64. Gems are plentiful but only 200 superb gems have been certified by PCGS. About 1 percent of all coins graded qualify as prooflike or deep mirror prooflike.

1885-O
Certified Populations and Check List
Mint State

Circ	MS-60	MS-61	MS-62	MS-63	MS-64	MS-65	MS-66	MS-67	MS-68
203	94	806	10,399	59,677	64,390	17,672	2,286	198	

Prooflike

Circ	MS-60	MS-61	MS-62	MS-63	MS-64	MS-65	MS-66	MS-67	MS-68
	13	47	234	780	621	207	27	1	

Deep Mirror Prooflike

Circ	MS-60	MS-61	MS-62	MS-63	MS-64	MS-65	MS-66	MS-67	MS-68
	23	44	178	530	568	209	35	1	

1885-S

Mintage 1,497,000

Certified Population. 8,769

Prooflike % 1.69

Deep Mirror Prooflike %. 0.01

The total mintage of the 1885-S is less than half that of the 1884-S and one quarter of the 1883-S. The reason behind this decline can be explained in two words: supply and demand. According to the Mint director's *Annual Report*, the San Francisco Mint had 32,029,467 dollar coins on hand but had only distributed 3,516,033 pieces by the end the fiscal year. With secure storage space becoming dear, the U.S. Mint had to shift much of its production east.

Despite the issue's low mintage, the 1885-S is considerably more plentiful than its S-Mint counterparts from the preceding two years. In circulated grades and in Mint State, collectors in the first half of the 20th century had ample opportunity to pick up an 1885-S if they so desired. However, those expecting the coin to remain cheap due to the great Treasury releases in the 1960s were in for a rude awakening, as this year's issue was not represented in any great number (a few bags here or there are all that's reported). By the middle of the 1960s the coin began to climb in value and it has never looked back.

In terms of quality, the 1885-S scarcely resembles the earlier S-Mint coins. Bagginess is part of the problem, but more so than that is mediocre mushy strikes. Were it not for the ample amount of frost, one might confuse this release for a New Orleans strike. Because of these problems, the average certified grade ranges from MS-62 to MS-64, with gems being scarce. Today the coin trades in the $200 to $320 range up to choice and above $1,600 in gem.

To date, only one coin has been attributed deep mirror prooflike by PCGS, it being graded MS-65. Prooflikes are scarce; the bulk grade from MS-62 to MS-64, which is in line with what one would expect considering the quality of the issue.

1885-S
Certified Populations and Check List
Mint State

Circ	MS-60	MS-61	MS-62	MS-63	MS-64	MS-65	MS-66	MS-67	MS-68
866	93	424	1,632	2,856	2,268	449	30	2	

Prooflike

Circ	MS-60	MS-61	MS-62	MS-63	MS-64	MS-65	MS-66	MS-67	MS-68
	2	10	24	51	52	8	1		

Deep Mirror Prooflike

Circ	MS-60	MS-61	MS-62	MS-63	MS-64	MS-65	MS-66	MS-67	MS-68
						1			

1886

Mintage 19,963,000

Certified Population. 103,272

Prooflike % 0.80

Deep Mirror Prooflike %. 0.76

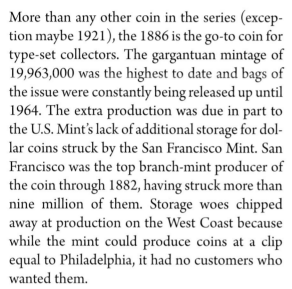

More than any other coin in the series (exception maybe 1921), the 1886 is the go-to coin for type-set collectors. The gargantuan mintage of 19,963,000 was the highest to date and bags of the issue were constantly being released up until 1964. The extra production was due in part to the U.S. Mint's lack of additional storage for dollar coins struck by the San Francisco Mint. San Francisco was the top branch-mint producer of the coin through 1882, having struck more than nine million of them. Storage woes chipped away at production on the West Coast because while the mint could produce coins at a clip equal to Philadelphia, it had no customers who wanted them.

Congress continued to play dumb on the matter, and offered little in the way of funding for massive new storage vaults for the burdensome coins. Even though the country already had enough Morgan dollars to last another hundred years, putting an end to the production of new coins was off the table. The Philadelphia and New Orleans mints also had to make up for the absence of production from Carson City, which was shuttered at the end of 1885. Its coinage was shipped to vaults back east—vaults already bursting at the seams themselves.

To add insult to injury, Congress authorized the issuing of Silver Certificates, redeemable in silver dollars. The reverse of the $5 certificate shows five Morgan dollars, the middle one being an 1886. The image was meant to entice Americans to support the use of the dollar coin, but the public rejected it in favor of paper money. This was not what Free Silver advocates had in mind.

So many were struck and so low was the demand in the 19th century that many 1886 dollars survived to the present day in Mint State. Hundreds if not thousands of bags survived the Pittman Act and served to frustrate coin speculators, in the 1950s and 1960s, who traveled to the Treasury cash window to buy mint-sewn bags. The 1886 was one of the dates found in quantity in the Continental-Illinois Bank hoard.

The coin barely sold over face value until the cost of bullion exceeded it. Then for the longest time the 1886 was considered a bullion coin, even in Mint State. The advent of certified third-party grading and the popularity of VAMs (the date has several minor die varieties) breathed new life into the 1886. Today the coin sells for well over its bullion value in all circulated grades and carries a significant premium starting at MS-65. The typical Mint State example grades MS-62 to MS-65.

The percentage of prooflike and deep mirror prooflike coins from this issue are low, even considering the large population of certified coins. PLs and DMPLs make up less than 1 percent of the total PCGS graded population. Gems for both types are scarce.

1886
Certified Populations and Check List

Mint State

Circ	MS-60	MS-61	MS-62	MS-63	MS-64	MS-65	MS-66	MS-67	MS-68
739	101	718	7,112	35,136	40,445	14,555	2,484	274	3

Prooflike

Circ	MS-60	MS-61	MS-62	MS-63	MS-64	MS-65	MS-66	MS-67	MS-68
	3	20	121	283	274	100	20	1	

Deep Mirror Prooflike

Circ	MS-60	MS-61	MS-62	MS-63	MS-64	MS-65	MS-66	MS-67	MS-68
	7	33	79	257	247	133	27		

1886-O

Mintage 10,710,000

Certified Population. 5,123

Prooflike % 0.14

Deep Mirror Prooflike %. 0.27

With a mintage of more than 10 million, you'd think the 1886-O, like its cousin from Philadelphia, would be a common sight in Mint State. But as we've seen before, mintage totals don't tell the whole story. In the case of the 1886-O, a large percentage of that total mintage is unaccounted for. Mint-sewn bags never materialized in quantity in the 1950s and 1960s. One obvious possibility is that most of the issue was melted under the Pittman Act of 1918.

The total number of remaining Mint State examples has become somewhat better known, after 40 years of third-party grading and the publication of population reports like PCGS CoinFacts™. To date 5,123 1886-O dollars have been graded by PCGS, with 3,100 of these having been circulated. This leaves only a few hundred Mint State coins to satisfy hundreds of thousands of Morgan dollar collectors.

Dealers have always understood that the issue is scarce. In the 1960 edition of the *Red Book*, for instance, the 1886-O was the 20th (out of 100) highest-priced issue of the series in Uncirculated condition. When numerical grading became an industry standard in the late 1970s and early 1980s, collectors and dealers began to realize just how few Uncirculated examples existed, especially choice coins and gems. In the 2014 *Red Book*, a "generic" MS-60 is the series' 19th-highest-priced issue, while in MS-65 the coin jumps to the 6th-highest-priced in the set—a *bona fide* conditional rarity!

Under the Loupe: I've personally graded the MS-67DMPL 1886-O, and I can assure you it is all there. It's a monster coin with deep reflective mirrors and thick white cameo frosting on the devices. There's no doubt in my mind that this will be a one or two million-dollar coin someday.

1886-O
Certified Populations and Check List
Mint State

Circ	MS-60	MS-61	MS-62	MS-63	MS-64	MS-65	MS-66	MS-67	MS-68
3,100	178	356	689	556	221	2			

Prooflike

Circ	MS-60	MS-61	MS-62	MS-63	MS-64	MS-65	MS-66	MS-67	MS-68
		1	3	3					

Deep Mirror Prooflike

Circ	MS-60	MS-61	MS-62	MS-63	MS-64	MS-65	MS-66	MS-67	MS-68
	2	1	6	1	3			1	

1886-S

Mintage 750,000

Certified Population 6,239

Prooflike % 4.02

Deep Mirror Prooflike % 0.98

With the exception of 1887, all San Francisco issues for the remainder of the 1880s would have total mintages under a million. Throughout the duration of the series, San Francisco would strike one million or fewer coins a total of five times. Of those five issues, the 1886-S is relatively more affordable.

Q. David Bowers, in his book *Silver Dollars & Trade Dollars of the United States* (1993), recounts that an Uncirculated 1886-S sold for $26.50 in 1914.[17] Adjusting for inflation, the buyer purchased the coin for about $615.[18]

The biggest documented infusion of 1886-S dollars on the market came from the Redfield hoard, which John Love believes contained at least three mint-sewn bags. Most of the contents of these bags were sold in the late 1970s by Paramount International Coin Corporation, in plastic holders that resemble modern-day third-party grading company holders. Of course, Paramount was grading their own coins, so it can't be considered independent (and hence "third party")—but their use of numerical grading on sealed coin holders helped pave the way for the widespread adoption of the Sheldon grading scale.

The typical 1886-S dollar grades from MS-62 to MS-64. Gems are scarce. The issue is more commonly found in prooflike than deep mirror prooflike. Several of the Redfield hoard coins were said to have prooflike characteristics. The typical grade for these coins is in line with the general population, with the exception that PCGS has graded but one DMPL MS-65.

1886-S
Certified Populations and Check List

Mint State

Circ	MS-60	MS-61	MS-62	MS-63	MS-64	MS-65	MS-66	MS-67	MS-68
1,058	77	282	1,148	1,774	1,262	288	34	4	

Prooflike

Circ	MS-60	MS-61	MS-62	MS-63	MS-64	MS-65	MS-66	MS-67	MS-68
	2	14	50	92	67	22	4		

Deep Mirror Prooflike

Circ	MS-60	MS-61	MS-62	MS-63	MS-64	MS-65	MS-66	MS-67	MS-68
	2	1	15	21	21	1			

1887

Mintage	20,290,000
Certified Population.	130,037
Prooflike %	1.41
Deep Mirror Prooflike %.	0.75

Sounding like a broken phonograph, director of the Mint James P. Kimball pleaded with Congress once more to remedy the lack of secure storage facilities for surplus silver-dollar coinage. That there was insufficient demand to justify continued coinage under Bland-Allison was never in dispute by anyone whose political interests weren't served by the continued patronage of the Western state silver interests. But the Mint soldiered on, producing the overwhelming majority of the requisite number of dollars at the Philadelphia and New Orleans mints. San Francisco, the most modern of all four mint facilities, had little place to store unwanted Morgan dollars, so they were ordered to coin to demand.

The Philadelphia Mint reached its peak pre-1921 Morgan dollar production in 1887, minting 20,290,000 dollar coins. The issue is one of the most common surviving Morgan dollars in Mint State, but it is far from the most frequently submitted—that appellation goes to the 1881-S, with more than 230,000 coins submitted to PCGS.

For the longest time 1887 dollars were available at face value. Thousands of bags poured out of Treasury vaults. If you were a coin dealer traveling to Washington, D.C., in the 1960s to buy bags of dollar coins, the 1887 Philly strike was one issue you definitely didn't want to see. When the intrinsic value of silver surpassed the coin's face value, starting in the late 1960s, the 1887 became primarily a bullion coin, even in Mint State.

Scores of bags of this date were held by the Continental-Illinois Bank, and were purchased in the early 1980s by

RARCOA's Ed Milas. While most of the original Mint bags have been opened, it's possible that a few might still be stashed away in old collections.

The typical grade of an Uncirculated 1887 Morgan dollar is from MS-62 to MS-64. Gems are available at a slight premium, but are far less plentiful in MS-63 and MS-64. The quality of the issue is inconsistent overall, as dies were used well into very late die state (VLDS). Prooflike and deep mirror prooflike pieces, while representing a low percentage of the total number of graded coins, are available in sufficient numbers.

1887
Certified Populations and Check List
Mint State

Circ	MS-60	MS-61	MS-62	MS-63	MS-64	MS-65	MS-66	MS-67	MS-68
590	90	741	7,875	45,717	55,688	14,986	1,457	83	1

Prooflike

Circ	MS-60	MS-61	MS-62	MS-63	MS-64	MS-65	MS-66	MS-67	MS-68
	3	28	154	621	716	258	52	3	

Deep Mirror Prooflike

Circ	MS-60	MS-61	MS-62	MS-63	MS-64	MS-65	MS-66	MS-67	MS-68
	5	11	87	309	359	172	31		

1887-O

Mintage 11,550,000
Certified Population 10,309
Prooflike % 3.15
Deep Mirror Prooflike % 2.46

The New Orleans Mint produced 11,550,000 Morgan dollars in 1887, a record for the branch but a distant second to the Philadelphia Mint's concurrently prodigious output. The two mints would keep up the pace through 1890, when San Francisco would resume pressing coins at a rate similar to pre-1883 levels.

Still, the U.S. Treasury found only limited success distributing dollar coins struck in New Orleans and Philadelphia, despite the fact that the population density of the regions serviced by the two Eastern mints, which had long-established cities, covered the bulk of the United States' 59 million people.

Even though evidence suggests that bags of New Orleans entered the flow of commerce, the coins didn't see heavy use, and many of them ended up back in Mint bags to be stored in the vaults. They were common during the federal government's divestiture of Morgan dollar bags in the 1950s and 1960s.

A fair portion of this issue was likely melted in 1918, but

enough Uncirculated bags were released in the 1950s and 1960s to satisfy collector demand. The key to this issue is finding well-struck pieces (easier said than done) with minimal marks. The average grade of an Uncirculated 1887-O is from MS-62 to MS-64. Gems are scarce and only 12 coins to date have been graded MS-66 by PCGS.

Prooflike and deep mirror prooflike coins make up approximately 6 percent of the issue graded by PCGS, with DMPLs being slightly scarcer at 2.46 percent. Like brilliant Uncirculated 1887-O's, most cameos are heavily bag marked and abraded. The average grade of both designations is from MS-62 to MS-64.

1887-O
Certified Populations and Check List
Mint State

Circ	MS-60	MS-61	MS-62	MS-63	MS-64	MS-65	MS-66	MS-67	MS-68
643	109	418	1,908	3,812	2,526	305	9		

Prooflike

Circ	MS-60	MS-61	MS-62	MS-63	MS-64	MS-65	MS-66	MS-67	MS-68
	6	13	68	116	105	15	2		

Deep Mirror Prooflike

Circ	MS-60	MS-61	MS-62	MS-63	MS-64	MS-65	MS-66	MS-67	MS-68
	5	23	50	74	96	6	1		

1887-S

Mintage 1,771,000

Certified Population. 8,541

Prooflike % 1.21

Deep Mirror Prooflike %. 0.88

The 1887-S was one of the premium issues found in quantity in the Redfield hoard—8,000 to 10,000 coins, by John Love's count. Several of them would be considered gems if judged by today's standards.

Paramount, the company that handled the distribution of most of the pieces from this date, wisely seized upon the marketing opportunity that numerical grading provided when selling the hoard. This innovation allowed the company to maximize profits on a coin-by-coin basis. The coins were divided into three categories: MS-60, which came in dark blue holders; MS-65, which came in maroon holders; and MS-70, which came in green holders. (The assigned grades bore little relation to the grades given to the same coins by PCGS at a later date.)

Use of the term *MS-70* before the era of third-party grading was much different than it is now. In 1959, legendary dealer Abe Kosoff described portions of the famous James Sloss collection as having large cents that grade MS-70![19] Still, the concept of numerical grading was gaining traction in numismatic and investment circles, and the proliferation of Paramount holders greatly altered the grading landscape in the United States.

The effects of the Redfield 1887-S on the value of the rest of the issue are real but did not drop the issue into the realm of the common-date Morgan.

In 1971, the issue traded at $17.50 and held close to this price until the GSA sales ignited frenzied collector interest in the entire Morgan dollar series. By 1974 the price of a Mint State 1887-S had more than doubled, standing at $36.50. It then fell to $27 at the beginning of the distribution of the Redfield hoard, with MS-65 examples holding at $37.50.

In other words, collectors with high-quality pieces did not suffer a decline in value with the release of the Redfield coins. Those with generic pieces didn't suffer for long, either. MS-60s were selling for $117.50 by the end of the decade, while MS-65s traded at $260.00.

Adjusting for inflation, today the 1887-S is affordable and underrated. Quality is the big drawback, since most examples are scarred with bag marks—evidence, perhaps, that the coins were routinely and carelessly moved around before the Treasury released them. As a result, finding coins with clean-enough surfaces to grade MS-65 is difficult.

The issue also yields few prooflike or deep mirror prooflike coins. Combined, the two populations comprise less than 2 percent of the certified total, and PCGS has graded only one of them—a DMPL—at MS-65.

1887-S
Certified Populations and Check List
Mint State

Circ	MS-60	MS-61	MS-62	MS-63	MS-64	MS-65	MS-66	MS-67	MS-68
1,044	115	460	1,818	2,732	1,818	350	26		

Prooflike

Circ	MS-60	MS-61	MS-62	MS-63	MS-64	MS-65	MS-66	MS-67	MS-68
		7	22	49	25				

Deep Mirror Prooflike

Circ	MS-60	MS-61	MS-62	MS-63	MS-64	MS-65	MS-66	MS-67	MS-68
	2	8	17	25	22	1			

1888

Mintage 19,183,000

Certified Population. 36,585

Prooflike % 1.12

Deep Mirror Prooflike %. 0.95

In 1888 the Philadelphia Mint struck more than 72 million coins, the majority of which were concentrated in three denominations: the cent (37+ million), the nickel (10+ million), and the Morgan dollar (19+ million). The Morgan dollar continued to be struck without any apparent need for additional coinage (other than the demands of the Bland-Allison Act), but the Treasury Department did find a way to store at least a portion of the excess coinage.

The 1888 Philadelphia-strike Morgan dollar exhibits the series-typical range of quality. Fully struck early-die-state examples exist, but are largely outnumbered by weakly struck pieces made from worn dies or struck at inadequate pressure. The average grade for Uncirculated examples is in the MS-63 to MS-64 range.

Prooflike and deep mirror prooflike coins for this issue are decidedly scarce, and grades mirror those of brilliant Uncirculated dollars.

What if? For present-day numismatists, the idea of the government producing unwanted coins at an industrial scale is nothing new. In recent memory we have three such coins produced by the millions and practically uncirculated: the Susan B. Anthony, golden Sacagawea, and golden Presidential dollars.

Starting in 1979, the United States coined a small-format dollar honoring Susan B. Anthony. Derisively called "Carter's Quarter" or, even worse, "the J.C. Penny," the Anthony dollar, like the Morgan dollar, was never enthusiastically accepted by the American people. But unlike the Morgan, which had intrinsic worth, the Susan B. Anthony dollar was a base-metal coin that cost mere pennies to produce.

In 1982, with no demand for the coin and hundreds of millions of them stored in vaults, the Reagan administration ended the program. It wasn't until the late 1990s that the Treasury projected that it might exhaust its supply of dollars.[20] Like the Morgan dollar, which also experienced a 17-year hiatus, the Susan B. Anthony was struck for one last year, in 1999—a stopgap measure until the Sacagawea golden-dollar series could be released in 2000.

One can only wonder what President Ronald Reagan would have done had he been elected in 1888 instead of Benjamin Harrison (a silver supporter). Would the Morgan dollar series have come to an abrupt end?

1888
Certified Populations and Check List
Mint State

Circ	MS-60	MS-61	MS-62	MS-63	MS-64	MS-65	MS-66	MS-67	MS-68
266	53	374	3,131	14,175	13,811	3,345	655	18	

Prooflike

Circ	MS-60	MS-61	MS-62	MS-63	MS-64	MS-65	MS-66	MS-67	MS-68
	2	14	49	137	147	48	11		

Deep Mirror Prooflike

Circ	MS-60	MS-61	MS-62	MS-63	MS-64	MS-65	MS-66	MS-67	MS-68
	3	11	59	95	125	47	8	1	

1888-O

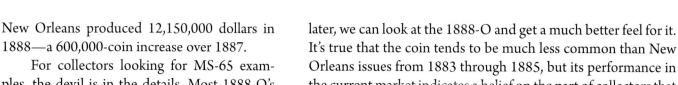

Mintage 12,150,000

Certified Population......... 20,985

Prooflike % 3.41

Deep Mirror Prooflike %..... 2.46

New Orleans produced 12,150,000 dollars in 1888—a 600,000-coin increase over 1887.

For collectors looking for MS-65 examples, the devil is in the details. Most 1888-O's are poorly struck, and some Uncirculated examples are so weak that they could never even qualify as gem! That alone is enough of a strike against the 1888-O, but the issue was also shipped from New Orleans to Washington, D.C., where a significant number of bags were stored until they were all handed out by 1964.

Dealers and marketers have debated whether the 1888-O should be considered a common-date coin or if it is, in fact, underrated. In the 1970s the issue was heavily promoted as a great "investor-quality" coin. Now, 40 years

later, we can look at the 1888-O and get a much better feel for it. It's true that the coin tends to be much less common than New Orleans issues from 1883 through 1885, but its performance in the current market indicates a belief on the part of collectors that the 1888-O is still somewhat common.

The typical 1888-O Morgan dollar grades between MS-63 and MS-64. This has as much to do with strike as it does surface quality. Premium pricing is the norm for examples with good eye appeal. Prooflike and deep mirror prooflike coins are semiscarce, but rare in MS-65 or above.

Hot Lips: A rare and impressive obverse doubled die exists. Van Allen and Mallis call the coin VAM 4 (Doubled Head), and describe the variety as the strongest doubled obverse of the Morgan series. It commands a significant premium, and is almost unheard of in Mint State.

1888-O
Certified Populations and Check List
Mint State

Circ	MS-60	MS-61	MS-62	MS-63	MS-64	MS-65	MS-66	MS-67	MS-68
528	46	312	2,029	7,748	7,055	1,807	229		

Prooflike

Circ	MS-60	MS-61	MS-62	MS-63	MS-64	MS-65	MS-66	MS-67	MS-68
	9	27	76	238	265	92	8		

Deep Mirror Prooflike

Circ	MS-60	MS-61	MS-62	MS-63	MS-64	MS-65	MS-66	MS-67	MS-68
	3	14	58	166	209	62	4		

1888-S

Mintage 657,000

Certified Population. 6,746

Prooflike % 2.70

Deep Mirror Prooflike %. 2.43

San Francisco produced 657,000 Morgan dollars in 1888, which is 93,000 fewer than that mint's previous low, in 1886. The coin market treats both issues roughly the same, putting them in a category of semi-scarce Morgan dollars, but the premiums offered for these two issues have more to do with what survives today and not their mintages.

The discovery of significant quantities in the Redfield hoard affected public perception of the low-mintage 1888-S. John Love believes the hoard yielded about 10,000 examples of the 1888-S, but the real number could be higher.

Still, the Redfield coins were dispersed more than 40 years ago, and while the 1888-S does appear regularly at auctions and coin shows, it's not a coin that's casually available in roll quantities or greater.

Furthermore, the issue shows evidence of frequent moving in original mint bags, which means heavy bag marks are the norm. The total surviving population of MS-65 coins may well be under 1,000. MS-62 is the average grade.

Prooflike and deep mirror prooflike examples are scarce, and downright rare in gem. PCGS has graded fewer than 200 in each classification. Together, PLs and DMPLs make up a little more than 5 percent of the total coins graded from this issue.

1888-S
Certified Populations and Check List
Mint State

Circ	MS-60	MS-61	MS-62	MS-63	MS-64	MS-65	MS-66	MS-67	MS-68
984	86	306	1,160	2,115	1,448	279	20	2	

Prooflike

Circ	MS-60	MS-61	MS-62	MS-63	MS-64	MS-65	MS-66	MS-67	MS-68
	2	6	37	66	67	3	1		

Deep Mirror Prooflike

Circ	MS-60	MS-61	MS-62	MS-63	MS-64	MS-65	MS-66	MS-67	MS-68
	2	9	34	73	43	3			

1889

Mintage 21,726,000

Certified Population. 32,648

Prooflike % 0.91

Deep Mirror Prooflike %. 0.79

In 1889 the federal government made headway in solving the Mint's long-standing shortage of secure and sufficient space to store all the millions of non-distributed silver dollars struck since 1878. In the first year of Benjamin Harrison's administration, a new steel-lined vault came online, providing for the storage of up to 85 million silver dollars.[21] The Philadelphia Mint also was able to transfer 42 million silver dollars to the Treasury in Washington, D.C. This development provided some much-needed breathing room for the superintendent of the Philadelphia Mint, who was tasked in 1889 to strike a record number of Morgan dollars.

To strike more than 21 million dollar coins, Philadelphia coiners pushed dies to the limit. The result is an issue that swings wildly from well-struck, early-die-state examples with beautiful luster, to very-late-die-state pieces that demonstrate a lack of detail and exhibit heavy flow lines and distortion.

Due to this issue's high mintage (the highest in the series until the 1921-P), the coin has always been considered common, even though the date turns up considerably less frequently than the early San Francisco issues. Bags of 1889s steadily trickled out of the Treasury in the 1950s and 1960s. Still more coins turned up in the 1970s after numerous bags of the date were discovered in the LaVere Redfield hoard. Amazingly, the Continental-Illinois Bank hoard, which featured a number of common P- and O-Mint coins, did not have appreciable quantities of 1889-P's.

Today, the 1889 is regularly offered and is a go-to date for type-set collectors.

The typical Uncirculated 1889 grade is from MS-62 to MS-64. Gems are the minority, with fewer than 2,000 certified by PCGS. A sole MS-68, blazing white, formerly belonged to Jack Lee.

As readily available as Mint State examples are, prooflike and deep mirror prooflike examples are among the scarcest for Philadelphia-struck Morgans.

Three You Later: 1889 saw the passing into history of the nickel three-cent piece. The coin, which debuted in the final year of the Civil War, was the de facto replacement of the silver trime of 1851 to 1873. The Philadelphia Mint closed out the series by minting 18,125 three-cent pieces plus 3,436 Proofs.

1889
Certified Populations and Check List
Mint State

Circ	MS-60	MS-61	MS-62	MS-63	MS-64	MS-65	MS-66	MS-67	MS-68
1,100	96	492	4,449	14,129	9,853	1,757	213	4	1

Prooflike

Circ	MS-60	MS-61	MS-62	MS-63	MS-64	MS-65	MS-66	MS-67	MS-68
		10	69	119	68	29	1		

Deep Mirror Prooflike

Circ	MS-60	MS-61	MS-62	MS-63	MS-64	MS-65	MS-66	MS-67	MS-68
	3	15	41	75	89	32	3		

1889-CC

Mintage	350,000
Certified Population	5,924
Prooflike %	1.28
Deep Mirror Prooflike %	2.58

After being shuttered as a coinage facility for three years (used in the meantime only for assaying and storage), the Carson City Mint was reactivated in July 1889. Before the mint could resume coinage operations, however, it required repairs to its structure and machinery. It also needed new officers and technicians. President Benjamin Harrison appointed Carson City resident Samuel C. Wright to resurrect the dormant facility by making him the new superintendent.

Wright was a colorful character in his own right, well known around town as Carson City's sole undertaker. Most of Carson City liked the man, with one notable exception. A journalist from the Virginia City *Territorial Enterprise* newspaper excoriated Wright for profiteering and overcharging the bereaved people of Carson City for his services. That journalist was Samuel Clemens, better known as author Mark Twain.

Superintendent Wright's administration ran through August 1892, when he died suddenly from a heart condition.

The number of dollars struck at Carson City in 1889 was low even by Carson City Mint standards. This was due to the fact that the mint wasn't fully operational until October 10. It also struck just under 31,000 double eagles, resulting in a coin that's considered a semi-common issue for the series.

Because the 1889-CC is one of the most coveted issues in the Morgan series, counterfeit coins were commonly passed in the 1970s and 1980s. Third-party authentication has helped the hobby clamp down on the problem and it's *strongly* advised that you only purchase certified examples of this date.

The average Uncirculated grade of the 1889-CC is MS-63. Circulated examples run the gamut from Good to About Uncirculated. Prooflikes and deep mirror prooflikes are scarce, which is atypical for Carson City Morgan dollars.

Needle in the Haystack: A single 1889-CC dollar was found in the government's holdings of Carson City dollars when the GSA began marketing the coins in 1972. It was made available in the Mixed CC offerings.

1889-CC
Certified Populations and Check List
Mint State

Circ	MS-60	MS-61	MS-62	MS-63	MS-64	MS-65	MS-66	MS-67	MS-68
5,416	16	53	88	76	30	1			1

Prooflike

Circ	MS-60	MS-61	MS-62	MS-63	MS-64	MS-65	MS-66	MS-67	MS-68
1	6	12	23	26	8				

Deep Mirror Prooflike

Circ	MS-60	MS-61	MS-62	MS-63	MS-64	MS-65	MS-66	MS-67	MS-68
	9	26	56	47	15				

1889-O

Mintage 11,875,000

Certified Population 6,746

Prooflike % 2.70

Deep Mirror Prooflike % 2.43

The New Orleans Mint produced only Morgan dollars in 1889, and the result of this hard work was almost 12 million weakly struck and lifeless coins. To make matters worse, careless handling over the years put most of the surviving Uncirculated examples in the lower echelons of Mint State. For a branch mint not known for consistently striking attractive coins, 1889-O represents a special achievement in lackluster coinage.

Literally, since most examples lack any semblance of nice luster.

A number of pieces, as many as a couple million, were distributed in the 19th century. Many circulated examples survive in grades ranging from Good to About Uncirculated. Several million more were likely melted by authority of the Pittman Act. Thousands of coins were released by the Treasury Department in the 1950s and 1960s. It's believed that as many as

70,000 to 80,000 examples might survive in Mint State; however, certified populations are small and could point to a survival rate a little lower than commonly believed.

Even with so many weakly struck pieces, you can still find a coin with great eye appeal that outperforms other coins in the same grade. Look for early-die-state examples with strong strikes and minimal abrasions.

In Uncirculated grades, the 1889-O tends to be MS-62 to MS-64. Gems are rare, with only 11 pieces earning an MS-66 from PCGS. Prooflike and deep mirror prooflike examples are also scarce.

A Cool Clashed Die: Typographical die clashes have always caught the attention of collectors. One rare 1889-O variety referred to in Van Allen and Mallis's *Comprehensive Catalog and Encyclopedia of Morgan & Peace Dollars* (1991, 4th edition) as VAM 1A2 features an E underneath the eagle's second tail feather. The wayward E is part of Liberty's coronet on the obverse. The E was transferred to the reverse during a die-clash episode where the hammer and anvil dies accidentally came into contact with each other.

1889-O
Certified Populations and Check List

Mint State

Circ	MS-60	MS-61	MS-62	MS-63	MS-64	MS-65	MS-66	MS-67	MS-68
856	59	284	1,218	2,058	1,562	152	10		

Prooflike

Circ	MS-60	MS-61	MS-62	MS-63	MS-64	MS-65	MS-66	MS-67	MS-68
		6	19	32	23	10	1		

Deep Mirror Prooflike

Circ	MS-60	MS-61	MS-62	MS-63	MS-64	MS-65	MS-66	MS-67	MS-68
	2	9	34	73	43	3			

1889-S

Mintage 700,000

Certified Population. 8,500

Prooflike % 1.94

Deep Mirror Prooflike %. 0.72

The San Francisco Mint struck four denominations in 1889: the eagle, double eagle, dollar, and dime. Dimes comprised the largest share of the year's output at just under a million coins, and the mint's primary focus for the year was striking $19.75 million in gold coinage. Silver dollars were strictly a secondary concern.

1889 marked the third time in four years that the San Francisco Mint struck fewer than one million Morgan dollars. The shift in production to the East had less to do with San Francisco's ability to strike coins—it was the most technologically advanced mint the United States had—than it did with a lack of demand for the coin in the West and the subsequent storage problem.

The 1889-S is an enigma, in part, because some of the most prestigious collectors of the early 20th century thought it was a great rarity.

At least a small percentage of the coins circulated in the 19th century; the remainder went into long-term storage. A few bags that survived the Pittman Act entered the market in the 1930s and 1940s. It wasn't until the 1970s that the largest publicized release of bags occurred, when approximately 5,000 1889-S coins were identified as part of the Redfield hoard.

The price of the 1889-S was already on the rise by the time the Redfield coins were marketed, since the GSA sales generated unprecedented collector interest in the entire Morgan dollar series. Its inclusion in the hoard helped raise the profile of the 1889-S, making it more easily obtainable for the thousands of new collectors arriving on the scene. Today this issue is well dispersed.

The typical Uncirculated 1889-S dollar grades from MS-62 to MS-64, due mostly to the preservation of the coins in Mint bags. Strike is less of a factor because the 1889-S is a well-struck coin. Prooflike and deep mirror prooflike coins are rare for this release.

1889-S
Certified Populations and Check List
Mint State

Circ	MS-60	MS-61	MS-62	MS-63	MS-64	MS-65	MS-66	MS-67	MS-68
1,271	80	315	1,275	2,540	2,137	591	64	1	

Prooflike

Circ	MS-60	MS-61	MS-62	MS-63	MS-64	MS-65	MS-66	MS-67	MS-68
	6	15	43	56	38	5	2		

Deep Mirror Prooflike

Circ	MS-60	MS-61	MS-62	MS-63	MS-64	MS-65	MS-66	MS-67	MS-68
	3	3	14	17	19	3	2		

1890

Mintage 16,802,000

Certified Population 15,017

Prooflike % 1.86

Deep Mirror Prooflike % 1.75

By some estimates, only one sixth of all Morgan dollars struck were circulating in 1890.[22] The rest were either distributed only to flow immediately back to the government, or put directly into vaults after striking.

Not satisfied with the federal government's purchase of between $2 and $4 million dollars a month in silver—for the production of coins that most Americans didn't use in the first place—the silver-mining interests and their pet politicians built a coalition of laborers and farmers to push for yet another increase in federal silver purchasing. It was an early instance of what is nowadays called *astroturfing* (as opposed to a true grassroots movement).

The new dollars were stored in government vaults, which was nothing new, and Americans were given a new currency backed by silver dollars. The Sherman Silver Purchase Act called for two million ounces of silver to be struck into coin for one year, and after that, dollar production would be dependent on the need for the redemption of Treasury Notes.

As a matter of policy (and a fatal one at that) the Treasury opted to redeem the notes in either silver *or* gold. Unfortunately, the price ratio of silver to gold was in serious decline, having gone from 16:1 to 20:1 by the time the legislation was enacted. This gap would widen as speculators seized upon the opportunity and exchanged their overvalued silver dollars for the Treasury's undervalued gold.

It took three years but this comedy of errors nearly bankrupted the federal government. Banker J.P. Morgan, whose business interests were threatened by a different Sherman act (the Sherman Antitrust Act) came to Washington's aid and loaned the government some of the gold it needed to remain solvent during the Panic of 1893.

For Morgan dollar production, 1890 represents the peak during the Sherman Act era. All four mints struck significant numbers of silver dollars, led by Philadelphia, which struck just over 16.8 million. The issue was freely available in unopened Mint bags until banks and the Treasury stopped paying out silver dollars at face value.

As is normal for most Philadelphia issues, the typical grade of an 1890 dollar in Uncirculated condition is from MS-62 to MS-64. Gems are scarce due to bag marks. Only two examples have been certified MS-66 by PCGS.

Also, the coin is not particularly known for its prooflike and deep mirror prooflike examples.

1890
Certified Populations and Check List
Mint State

Circ	MS-60	MS-61	MS-62	MS-63	MS-64	MS-65	MS-66	MS-67	MS-68
684	91	486	3,038	6,139	3,596	440	1		

Prooflike

Circ	MS-60	MS-61	MS-62	MS-63	MS-64	MS-65	MS-66	MS-67	MS-68
	6	19	72	85	82	14	1		

Deep Mirror Prooflike

Circ	MS-60	MS-61	MS-62	MS-63	MS-64	MS-65	MS-66	MS-67	MS-68
	5	16	62	77	97	6			

1890-CC

Mintage 2,309,041

Certified Population 12,200

Prooflike % 3.60

Deep Mirror Prooflike % 6.62

The 1890-CC represents the peak of Carson City Morgan dollar production. For the first time, the much-maligned Nevada mint surpassed the two million mark. Still, production costs at Carson City were higher than at any other mint, in large part due to economies of scale, but also due to the cost of renovations after it was reopened in 1889.

Looking at the mintage, one might think that the 1890-CC is one of the more common Carson City dollars, but that's not the case.

While bags were distributed in the 1940s and 1950s, the market consumed the bulk of this material at that time. When the GSA announced its holdings in 1972, only 3,589 Uncirculated 1890-CC dollars were available for mail-bid orders. The coin was offered at an affordable (by GSA standards) $30 per coin, which amounts to $167 in today's dollars, and quickly sold out. The issue has not been seen in quantity since.

The quality of the typical Uncirculated 1890-CC dollar is above average, with the typical grade falling in the MS-62 to MS-64 range. Prooflikes and deep mirror prooflikes are readily available for those seeking them out, and certified DMPLs outnumber PLs.

The Tail Bar: A damaged die is responsible for one of the most visually striking Morgan dollar varieties, known as the VAM 4, or the "Tail Bar." It features a raised design element, visible to the naked eye, that extends from the bottom of the arrows to the top of the wreath on the reverse. Most known Tail Bars came out of Montana in the 1970s. They are highly collectible.

1890-CC
Certified Populations and Check List
Mint State

Circ	MS-60	MS-61	MS-62	MS-63	MS-64	MS-65	MS-66	MS-67	MS-68
2,170	155	588	2,245	3,376	2,135	274	10		

Prooflike

Circ	MS-60	MS-61	MS-62	MS-63	MS-64	MS-65	MS-66	MS-67	MS-68
	5	46	136	135	103	14			

Deep Mirror Prooflike

Circ	MS-60	MS-61	MS-62	MS-63	MS-64	MS-65	MS-66	MS-67	MS-68
	29	54	190	296	218	21			

1890-O

Mintage 10,701,000

Certified Population 11,115

Prooflike % 4.06

Deep Mirror Prooflike % 2.70

For the second straight year, the sole concern of the New Orleans Mint was the production of Morgan dollars. Over the course of the year the Louisiana branch struck 10.7 million dollar coins, second only to the 16.8 million struck in Philadelphia.

From a numismatic standpoint, the 1890-O is tough to get excited about. Aesthetically the coin is a mess, and while many New Orleans issues don't compare favorably to better-made pieces from Carson City and San Francisco (and, to a lesser extent, Philadelphia), it seems that this particular date suffers more than others.

The biggest problem is strike. The 1890-O has been called a "pancake" by some; for others,

the typical grade of a Mint State coin could best be described as "MS-45." That is, they come already rubbed and worn. Many could be confused with circulated pieces.

Often this strike issue can be seen in Liberty's hair around the ear. It can also be seen in the lack of granular detail on the cotton blossoms in Liberty's headdress. On the reverse, nearly all of the eagle's chest feathers can appear washed out. Some Mint State examples even exhibit friction in the eagle's center mass, from the top of its chest to the right about the arrows. Even the better strikes may exhibit some lightness of these details.

The typical Mint State 1890-O Morgan grades from MS-62 to MS-64. It's likely that fewer than 1,000 gems exist. Prooflike and deep mirror prooflike coins are available, but sadly they suffer from the same strike tendencies and are frequently baggy.

1890-O
Certified Populations and Check List

Mint State

Circ	MS-60	MS-61	MS-62	MS-63	MS-64	MS-65	MS-66	MS-67	MS-68
303	57	316	1,720	4,079	3,396	473	20		

Prooflike

Circ	MS-60	MS-61	MS-62	MS-63	MS-64	MS-65	MS-66	MS-67	MS-68
	8	17	85	172	143	25	1		

Deep Mirror Prooflike

Circ	MS-60	MS-61	MS-62	MS-63	MS-64	MS-65	MS-66	MS-67	MS-68
	2	7	35	101	137	17	1		

1890-S

Mintage	8,230,373
Certified Population	10,757
Prooflike %	2.18
Deep Mirror Prooflike %	1.09

With increased storage capacity in the form of new vaults paid for by the Sundry Civil Act of 1889, the San Francisco Mint returned to form as a major producer of Morgan dollars.

The 1890-S is one of the dates found in abundance in the Redfield hoard, and for the better part of the late 1970s and early 1980s many collectors were leery of large caches of Mint State examples hitting the market. It's been speculated that the hoard contained anywhere from 20,000 to 40,000 Mint State 1890-S dollars.

Whether the hoard actually contained 20 or more bags is not clear. Even if that's accurate, the number of present-day Morgan dollar col-lectors far exceeds such a quantity. This may not have been true in the days before the GSA sale, but credit is due to the hard-working numismatists of the 1970s and 1980s who understood the importance and potential of the series and helped grow that demand.

The people who handled the Redfield hoard at the time of its release (namely John Love, Robert Hughes, and Paramount International Coin Company) did a masterful job of introducing their Morgan dollar holdings into the market without oversaturating it. A clear sign of their success can be seen in the way the market now treats the Paramount Redfield dollar holder as a numismatic collectible in and of itself.

As for the 1890-S as a collectible dollar coin: the piece is typically attractive and lustrous, with full strike detail and good eye appeal. While not quite on par with the San Francisco Mint's early output, the 1890-S fresh off the coining presses acquitted itself quite nicely and was an attractive coin. That most fail to grade MS-64 or MS-65 is a result of bag marks.

Original bags probably contained as many as 10 or even 20 gems. However, the days of going through original bags is long gone and the dearth of high-quality raw pieces coming onto the market and making their way into certified holders means that an eruption of new gems is unlikely.

While many 1890-S dollars exhibit some prooflike tendencies, coins with enough cameo contrast and reflective properties to be considered true prooflike or deep mirror prooflike examples are scarce, making the 1890-S one of the tougher common dates for PLs and DMPLs.

1890-S
Certified Populations and Check List
Mint State

Circ	MS-60	MS-61	MS-62	MS-63	MS-64	MS-65	MS-66	MS-67	MS-68
941	84	352	1,708	3,541	2,954	683	137	6	

Prooflike

Circ	MS-60	MS-61	MS-62	MS-63	MS-64	MS-65	MS-66	MS-67	MS-68
	6	12	57	83	59	14	3		

Deep Mirror Prooflike

Circ	MS-60	MS-61	MS-62	MS-63	MS-64	MS-65	MS-66	MS-67	MS-68
	2	8	34	35	30	8			

1891

Mintage 8,693,556

Certified Population. 8,431

Prooflike % 1.16

Deep Mirror Prooflike %. 0.98

Two new laws affected the minting of Morgan dollars in 1891. The Sherman Silver Purchase Act of July 14, 1890, required the Treasury Department to purchase 4.5 million ounces of silver each month to mint dollar coins. The program was supported by wealthy mine owners, of course, but also by farmers and laborers, who believed that an increase in the money supply would help solve their monetary woes. Then there was the Trade Dollar Recoinage Act of March 3, 1891, which authorized the government to reclaim silver from the 7.69 million trade dollars it had on hand at the Treasury.

The reclaimed bullion provided much of the silver used to strike 1891 dollars. Essentially, if you have an 1891-P or 1891-O dollar, it probably used to be a trade dollar.

The 1891 Philly strike, once considered one of the most common Morgan dollars, turns out to be quite elusive in gem. Most Mint State examples are believed to fall between MS-60 and MS-62, although PCGS population reports indicate far more pieces in the MS-62 to MS-64 range. The oversampling of the higher Mint State grades in this issue is the result of collectors and investors screening for quality in the hopes of landing better grades.

In other words, the low population of 122 coins in MS-65 isn't for the lack of trying.

Prooflike and deep mirror prooflike coins are equally scarce, with no known gem examples.

An abrupt end to the Morgan dollar? The story of the Morgan dollar could have come to a close in 1891, as Congress authorized the director of the Mint to abandon George T. Morgan's design in favor of a new one.

In April, the Mint sent out a call for new designs, not just for the Morgan dollar, but also for the obverses of all the nation's silver subsidiary coinage. An award of $500 per design was offered and a deadline set for June 1.

On June 3, a panel of judges—including Charles Barber and an immensely talented sculptor named Augustus Saint-Gaudens—notified the director that none of the proposed designs were an improvement over existing ones. The Mint ended the competition, and in 1892 replaced Christian Gobrecht's long-running Liberty Seated designs on the dime, quarter, and half dollar with Barber's new Liberty Head and a heraldic eagle. The Morgan dollar remained unchanged.

1891
Certified Populations and Check List
Mint State

Circ	MS-60	MS-61	MS-62	MS-63	MS-64	MS-65	MS-66	MS-67	MS-68
738	86	415	2,058	3,020	1,808	122	2	1	

Prooflike

Circ	MS-60	MS-61	MS-62	MS-63	MS-64	MS-65	MS-66	MS-67	MS-68
1	3	11	32	30	21				

Deep Mirror Prooflike

Circ	MS-60	MS-61	MS-62	MS-63	MS-64	MS-65	MS-66	MS-67	MS-68
	2	8	24	27	22				

1891-CC

Mintage 1,618,000

Certified Population 15,299

Prooflike % 3.30

Deep Mirror Prooflike % 2.14

Carson City's production of Morgan dollars was 30 percent off its previous high-water mark of 2.3 million coins in 1890. Still, at about 1.6 million, the 1891-CC is one of the more readily available issues in the series. While a significant number were distributed in the 19th century, a good many bags were transported to San Francisco for storage. These coins were released at regular intervals through the 1950s.

A few more than five bags' worth of 1891-CC dollars remained in government hands by the time of the GSA sale. This allotment was offered at a minimum bid of $30 per coin in the June–July 1973 sale; it sold out. An additional cache of 1891-CC dollars, roughly the same size as what was offered in 1973, was found in the Redfield hoard. According to John Love, these were mostly lower-grade Uncirculated pieces, frequently marred by bag marks.

According to PCGS, the typical grade of a certified 1891-CC is from MS-62 to MS-64. Demand for choice Uncirculated or better-grade coins is stronger than the available supply. Gems are scarce and the issue is rarely seen in grades MS-66 or above. Prooflike and deep mirror prooflike coins are also scarce.

1891-CC
Certified Populations and Check List
Mint State

Circ	MS-60	MS-61	MS-62	MS-63	MS-64	MS-65	MS-66	MS-67	MS-68
1,600	322	971	2,965	4,809	3,242	531	25	1	

Prooflike

Circ	MS-60	MS-61	MS-62	MS-63	MS-64	MS-65	MS-66	MS-67	MS-68
	3	53	163	159	111	15	1		

Deep Mirror Prooflike

Circ	MS-60	MS-61	MS-62	MS-63	MS-64	MS-65	MS-66	MS-67	MS-68
	15	30	95	135	52	1			

1891-O

Mintage	7,954,529
Certified Population	10,757
Prooflike %	0.75
Deep Mirror Prooflike %	0.45

Like the 1891 Philly strike, New Orleans Morgans this year were made of bullion-reclaimed trade-dollar silver. The issue's mintage is just below that of the Philadelphia Mint, as 1891 marked the lowest Morgan dollar production total since the series debut in 1878. The fall-off in production was a taste of things to come.

Discounting a minority of attractive, well-struck pieces, numismatists have often remarked that the 1891-O issue contains some of New Orleans' least attractive coins. A considerable number have flat, unattractive rims caused by improper die spacing. This feature contributes to the coin's "un-realness." Also, most dollars were striking up without full detail, so it is speculated this was done in an attempt to compensate.

Collectors looking for an 1891-O have a lot to consider. The typical coin falls in the range of MS-62 to MS-64, but that's only part of the story. Gems are rare; so are brilliant, fully struck examples. Attractive coins exist in late die state. Nice toners in the MS-64 or MS-65 range dazzle in an issue not well known for its beauty. However, nearly every well-preserved Mint State example has some kind of flaw that needs to be accounted for and worked around.

Also, the 1891-O is one of the rarest issues in the whole Morgan dollar series for prooflike and deep mirror prooflike coins. With a PCGS certified population of less than 100 coins, there aren't nearly enough pieces on the market to satisfy demand. Only the issue's high mintage and the hope that more PL and DMPL coins might be found keep prices at their current levels.

1891-O
Certified Populations and Check List
Mint State

Circ	MS-60	MS-61	MS-62	MS-63	MS-64	MS-65	MS-66	MS-67	MS-68
767	62	286	1,128	2,142	1,425	92			

Prooflike

Circ	MS-60	MS-61	MS-62	MS-63	MS-64	MS-65	MS-66	MS-67	MS-68
	1	4	8	21	11				

Deep Mirror Prooflike

Circ	MS-60	MS-61	MS-62	MS-63	MS-64	MS-65	MS-66	MS-67	MS-68
		2	8	8	7	2			

1891-S

Mintage 5,296,000

Certified Population 7,992

Prooflike % 5.13

Deep Mirror Prooflike % 1.66

The 1891-S rounded out a balanced year of Morgan dollar production. It would be six years before San Francisco produced Morgan dollars in excess of 1891's total mintage. By that time, the United States of America would have suffered through one of the worst depressions of the 19th century, stepped back from the precipice of bankruptcy, and joined into the final battle between the Silverites and the Gold Bugs. But in 1891 that was all yet to come. In 1891, it was business as usual for the Mint and the U.S. economy.

The 1891-S was considered a common-date Morgan dollar for much of its life. It wasn't as plentiful as the 1881-S or 1886, but with relatively few specialists vying for what seemed like an immense inventory of coins, collectors and dealers paid little notice.

That changed after the transition from circulating silver to copper-nickel-clad coinage. The highly publicized GSA sales, coupled with a strong coin hobby in the 1970s, helped demand outstrip supply. After numerical grading came into prominence, demand for high-end coins far exceeded what was available. Even today, gem 1891-S Morgan dollars are scarce.

This is an attractive, well-struck issue. The typical Uncirculated piece grades from MS-62 to MS-64. Abrasions from careless storage plague the issue more than anything else.

John Love recalls five bags full of low-grade Uncirculated 1891-S Morgans being part of LaVere Redfield's hoard of silver dollars. Several of the Redfield coins exhibited prooflike tendencies, and, numerically speaking, prooflikes are well represented. Deep mirror prooflikes, on the other hand, are scarce. To date only four examples qualify as DMPL in gem.

1891-S
Certified Populations and Check List
Mint State

Circ	MS-60	MS-61	MS-62	MS-63	MS-64	MS-65	MS-66	MS-67	MS-68
738	61	260	1,298	2,607	1,993	423	65	6	

Prooflike

Circ	MS-60	MS-61	MS-62	MS-63	MS-64	MS-65	MS-66	MS-67	MS-68
	6	24	93	163	100	23	1		

Deep Mirror Prooflike

Circ	MS-60	MS-61	MS-62	MS-63	MS-64	MS-65	MS-66	MS-67	MS-68
	2	12	35	50	30	4			

Mintage 1,036,000
Certified Population 5,748
Prooflike % 1.64
Deep Mirror Prooflike % 1.20

The Barber era began in 1892, with new designs for the dime, quarter, and half dollar.

The country faced troubling political and economic headwinds: Midwestern farmers, most of them deeply in debt, began to fall behind and default on their mortgages. This undercut bank-operating resources, and investors, seeing no positive yield from mortgage paper, pulled out of the financial market. Railroad construction, a driver of economic growth since the end of the Civil War, slowed drastically. All of these problems, however, were masked by a fairly strong economy.[23]

1892 marked the first time in the Morgan dollar series that Philadelphia struck fewer coins than every one of its branch mints. It also marked the beginning of a precipitous decline in silver-dollar production that would last through 1896. The Sherman Act called for the increased coinage of silver dollars, but provided a limited window for that mandate. That window closed on June 30, 1891, the end of the 1890–1891 fiscal year.

In 1892 the Mint was producing Morgan dollars strictly to demand. Looking at the mintage, that demand was a fraction of historical production figures, which started with 22.5 million coins in 1878 and peaked at 38 million coins in 1890. For collectors, reduced production set the stage for many of the series' great rarities.

Mediocre strikes far outnumber well-struck examples from this issue. Because of this, the coins exhibit a wide range of eye appeal within any given grade. While gems are truly scarce, high-quality pieces exist in the lower register of the Mint State scale. Choose a coin with good luster and a full strike, especially in the central device, over coins that appear flat and suffer from multiple abrasions.

Prooflike and deep mirror prooflike pieces are rare, with only a few hundred accounted for. MS-65 is the top pop grade for both PL and DMPL designations and both number in the single digits. The typical grade of these premium strikes is MS-62 to MS-64, mirroring that of most brilliant Uncirculated examples.

1892
Certified Populations and Check List
Mint State

Circ	MS-60	MS-61	MS-62	MS-63	MS-64	MS-65	MS-66	MS-67	MS-68
801	45	202	848	1,764	1,395	263	4		

Prooflike

Circ	MS-60	MS-61	MS-62	MS-63	MS-64	MS-65	MS-66	MS-67	MS-68
	2	7	18	32	29	2			

Deep Mirror Prooflike

Circ	MS-60	MS-61	MS-62	MS-63	MS-64	MS-65	MS-66	MS-67	MS-68
	4	5	12	14	26	5			

1892-CC

Mintage 1,352,000

Certified Population 8,867

Prooflike % 4.96

Deep Mirror Prooflike % 1.89

A sizeable number of 1892-CC dollars circulated in the 19th century. The year's total Morgan dollar mintage of 1,352,000 meant that Carson City out-produced the Philadelphia Mint for the first time since the series began in 1878.

Undistributed bags of Carson City dollars wound up in San Francisco vaults, where they were gradually paid out through the 1940s, and according to an account published in Bowers's *Silver Dollars & Trade Dollars of the United States,* some 50 bags were released in 1955. Even with this distribution, the 1892-CC still fared better than most common-date Morgan dollars, selling for $6 per coin in 1960 and $45 apiece by 1970. These prices seem unbelievable today, when even circulated examples command prices approaching $800.

The final publicized release of 1892-CC dollars came in the mid-1970s, when some turned up in the Redfield hoard. John Love estimates that about 2,500 to 3,000 Uncirculated examples were among LaVere Redfield's vast accumulation. It was one of the better dates in the lot.

In terms of quality, the 1892-CC usually is well struck. In Mint State, the issue is often grade-limited by bag marks. Gems are scarce but most examples certified by PCGS fall in the MS-62 to MS-64 range. Several Redfield 1892-CCs show small counting-wheel marks—unsightly scratches imparted on a coin's surface by professional-grade coin-counting machines—on the high point of the cheek. If pronounced, PCGS labels these coins "damaged" and provides a details grade, which informs the collector of the quality of the coin's features but does not render a proper grade.

Many 1892-CCs found in the Redfield hoard exhibit characteristics bordering on prooflike. A lot of them qualified for the designation, which is why prooflike examples make up nearly five percent of the total certified population. Deep mirror prooflikes are much more scarce.

1892-CC
Certified Populations and Check List
Mint State

Circ	MS-60	MS-61	MS-62	MS-63	MS-64	MS-65	MS-66	MS-67	MS-68
1,853	134	492	1,618	2,195	1,617	324	24	2	

Prooflike

Circ	MS-60	MS-61	MS-62	MS-63	MS-64	MS-65	MS-66	MS-67	MS-68
	27	51	138	133	81	10			

Deep Mirror Prooflike

Circ	MS-60	MS-61	MS-62	MS-63	MS-64	MS-65	MS-66	MS-67	MS-68
	12	26	60	41	27	2			

1892-O

Mintage 2,744,000
Certified Population. 6,446
Prooflike % 0.19
Deep Mirror Prooflike %. 1.66

The 1892-O is the most common of the 1892 Morgan dollars, unless you're looking for a prooflike or deep mirror prooflike piece (see below). A number of coins from this issue circulated in the 19th century, but a majority of the issue was held in government vaults and either melted under the Pittman Act or released by the Treasury in various increments until a deluge of New Orleans Mint dollars was released in late 1962.

As is often the case with New Orleans–struck Morgan dollars, quality varies wildly.

Most Mint State pieces are poorly struck and lack definition in Liberty's hair and on the eagle's chest. Even if these coins are relatively free of abrasions, collectors tend to ignore them in favor of the much less common sharply struck example.

That the 1892-O is so weak in regards to strike is one of the main reasons why there are so few gems. An assortment of beautifully struck gems belonging to a dealer from Wisconsin is said to be the source of many of the issue's finest coins. According to Heritage Auctions co-chairman and CEO Steve Ivy, a number of these coins were shown to him at the ANA Mid-Winter convention in February 1978.[24] Bowers also refers to this bag of coins in his *Encyclopedia*.

The 1892-O is one of the hardest Morgan dollars to find prooflike or deep mirror prooflike. As a matter of fact, it's one of the series' real stoppers in PL and DMPL. Twelve have been certified prooflike by PCGS, while only seven have been certified as deep mirror prooflike.

1892-O
Certified Populations and Check List
Mint State

Circ	MS-60	MS-61	MS-62	MS-63	MS-64	MS-65	MS-66	MS-67	MS-68
566	53	190	1,056	2,473	1,923	161	4	1	

Prooflike

Circ	MS-60	MS-61	MS-62	MS-63	MS-64	MS-65	MS-66	MS-67	MS-68
		1	1	6	4				

Deep Mirror Prooflike

Circ	MS-60	MS-61	MS-62	MS-63	MS-64	MS-65	MS-66	MS-67	MS-68
				4		3			

1892-S

Mintage 1,200,000

Certified Population......... 3,693

Prooflike % 0.14

Deep Mirror Prooflike %..... 0.03

It's hard to say that an issue that routinely trades for more than $100,000 is underrated, but the 1892-S is a coin that's rarely found in Mint State, since they were either released in the 19th century or melted in 1918. Only the 1893-S is harder to find in Uncirculated grades.

For most collectors, these elusive Uncs are out of reach, which is why demand for coins in the About Uncirculated band is always high. AU-58s (examples referred to as *sliders* by the last generation of numismatists) can fetch upward of $16,000. Compare this to the price of an 1892-S in AU-50 ($1,800), and you see a lot of wishful thinking on the part of collectors hoping to get lucky and upgrade. That must've been on one bidder's mind in 2011, when an example sold at a Heritage auction for $32,200.

In Very Fine to Extremely Fine, the 1892-S becomes an affordable coin, behaving like you would expect for a 19th-century issue with a mintage in excess of one million. Pieces in this range sell for $150 and up. We settle at $250+ for our circulated grade guidance because we believe that most readers would prefer a coin in EF or AU.

Prooflike and deep mirror prooflike coins are nearly unheard of for this issue. This is due to the tiny pool of Mint State examples, which makes it impossible for us to know how often these frosted coins appeared in the original mintage. Considering that PCGS has graded fewer than 65 coins in Mint State, it's fortunate that six PL and DMPL Morgan dollars even exist. For most PL and DMPL collectors who can afford to buy six-figure Morgans, the 1892-S is as close to a stopper as the series gets.

1892-S
Certified Populations and Check List
Mint State

Circ	MS-60	MS-61	MS-62	MS-63	MS-64	MS-65	MS-66	MS-67	MS-68
3,628	1	6	24	5	9	5	3	5	1

Prooflike

Circ	MS-60	MS-61	MS-62	MS-63	MS-64	MS-65	MS-66	MS-67	MS-68
	2			3					

Deep Mirror Prooflike

Circ	MS-60	MS-61	MS-62	MS-63	MS-64	MS-65	MS-66	MS-67	MS-68
		1							

Mintage	389,000
Certified Population.	6,051
Prooflike %	0.05
Deep Mirror Prooflike %.	0.08

Silver and the Panic of 1893: Despite being strong just the year before, the American economy plunged into a state of disarray that economists call the Panic of 1893. The reasons were myriad: overproduction of goods, overbuilding of railroads, deflation, unwieldy debt in the agriculture sector, economic weakness abroad, and reduced income on imports as a result of the McKinley Tariff of 1890. But as far as the public at large was concerned, the *prima facie* cause of the panic was the Sherman Silver Purchase Act of 1890.

On its surface, one can see why silver was such an easy scapegoat. The Treasury had too much unwanted silver coinage in its vaults. Foreign banks and investors were extracting gold specie payment with surgical precision. And finally, the global supply of silver dwarfed its dwindling demand. The imbalance between the values of silver and gold had made the 16:1 ratio untenable.

To deal with the crisis, President Grover Cleveland called for a special session of Congress, and on August 8 they repealed the Sherman Silver Purchase Act. The crisis continued unabated, leading to additional governmental attempts at remedy. By 1895, the Treasury's gold supply would be so depleted that the government would take banker J.P. Morgan up on his offer of a loan.

Minted to Demand: Even without the repeal, 1893 mintages would have been off from the previous year. The Sherman Silver Purchase Act, while mandating the purchase of more silver than Bland-Allison, provided some relief insofar as the Mint only had to strike up dollars to back Coin Notes. The slowing of the economy would have continued to slow demand for the notes.

In Philadelphia, Morgan dollar production was an afterthought. A mere 378,000 were struck by year's end—a far cry from the millions minted in previous years. From a quality perspective, the coins are on a par with the better Philadelphia issues, revealing beautiful luster, light bag marks, and strike quality that ranges from average to above average. The typical coin in Mint State (based on PCGS's population report) is from MS-62 to MS-64. Gems are five times scarcer than MS-64 examples; only four pieces have graded MS-66.

Of all of the 1893 issues, the Philly strike was readily available through the 1960s, as coins were steadily released by the Treasury in bags at face value. The Redfield hoard contained a couple of bags of the date, and one is believed to have sold before A-Mark purchased the hoard in 1976. John Love remembers finding one bag in 1959.

As was the case with the 1892-S, the 1893 is another stopper for those looking to assemble a complete collection of Morgan dollars in either prooflike or deep mirror prooflike. To date, PCGS has graded just three that qualify as PL and five that earned a DMPL designation. These pieces are all lower-grade coins, which is why, relative to their scarcity, their values are low.

1893
Certified Populations and Check List
Mint State

Circ	MS-60	MS-61	MS-62	MS-63	MS-64	MS-65	MS-66	MS-67	MS-68
2,431	47	204	750	1,223	1,183	201	4		

Prooflike

Circ	MS-60	MS-61	MS-62	MS-63	MS-64	MS-65	MS-66	MS-67	MS-68
	2		1						

Deep Mirror Prooflike

Circ	MS-60	MS-61	MS-62	MS-63	MS-64	MS-65	MS-66	MS-67	MS-68
	1	3	1						

1893-CC

Mintage 677,000

Certified Population. 6,158

Prooflike % 3.46

Deep Mirror Prooflike %. 0.11

The Mint at Carson City hummed along in 1893, turning out $808,000 in gold coins and $677,000 in silver Morgan dollars. It was the last year the Nevada facility would produce coins; the secretary of the Treasury ordered the facility to close on June 1, 1893, thus ending a colorful and important era in U.S. numismatic history.

A few Morgan dollars from this issue found their way into circulation in the 20th century, but not enough were preserved to satisfy modern demand. One solitary example was found to reside in the GSA hoard.

The best shot the market had for an infusion of newly discovered 1893-CC dollars came

when a couple of bags turned up in the Redfield hoard in the mid-1970s. Many of these coins were tragically ruined when inspectors ran the coins through a coin-counting machine, which imparted noticeable scrapes on the high points of Liberty's cheek. Having seen many in hand, rest assured that the damage done to these coins precludes the possibility of anything other than a details grade—which is a shame from a preservation perspective, but of course it only adds to the issue's collectability.

In Mint State the 1893-CC is usually found in the lower end of the spectrum, grading MS-61 to MS-64. Gems are nearly unheard of due to the fact that this issue is one of the weaker-struck Carson City Morgans and almost all of the surviving

Uncirculated coins are moderately to heavily bag marked.

In prooflike and deep mirror prooflike, the 1893-CC is scarce. While not the stopper that other recent-date issues are, obtaining a PL or DMPL 1893-CC is still a challenging and expensive proposition for the collector. Most known examples are bag marked. One PL is certified MS-65 by PCGS. Only seven coins meet PCGS's standards for DMPL, with the two best grading MS-64.

1893-CC
Certified Populations and Check List
Mint State

Circ	MS-60	MS-61	MS-62	MS-63	MS-64	MS-65	MS-66	MS-67	MS-68
2,663	213	487	1,043	1,006	515	10	1		

Prooflike

Circ	MS-60	MS-61	MS-62	MS-63	MS-64	MS-65	MS-66	MS-67	MS-68
	60	04	65	22	1	1			

Deep Mirror Prooflike

Circ	MS-60	MS-61	MS-62	MS-63	MS-64	MS-65	MS-66	MS-67	MS-68
			3	2	2				

1893-O

Mintage 300,000
Certified Population. 3,647
Prooflike % 0.44
Deep Mirror Prooflike %. 0.38

300,000 Morgan dollars were struck at the New Orleans Mint in January 1893. After they finished with silver dollars, the coiners took up the work of striking 127,000 gold coins and a little more than $1.7 million in Barber halves, quarters, and dimes. On June 1, coinage was suspended for the remainder of the year.

The 1893-O is the second-scarcest New Orleans issue in the Morgan dollar series. It is by mintage 25 percent scarcer than the 1895-O, but in Mint State it's seven times more common. In circulated grades, however, both issues are considered equally scarce.

As recently as the mid-20th century, dealers didn't recognize this. It wasn't until the 1960s, when the coin failed to turn up in the government's inventory, that its price began to rise appreciably.

Collectors are attracted to this issue in both circulated and Uncirculated grades, as evidenced by the significant premiums the coin fetches in grades as low as Very Good. The $300+ circulated price listed below is the going rate for an example in Very

Fine. Expect to pay upwards of $1,000 for a high-end About Uncirculated example. In Mint State, the thousand or so pieces that remain tend to be heavily bag-marked and exhibit mediocre strike quality. The typical grade falls between MS-61 and MS-63.

The issue is another in a handful of stoppers for collectors of prooflike and deep mirror prooflike Morgans. Dispersal is fairly evenly split between the two attributions, but the ultimate 1893-O is the top-pop MS-66PL that once belonged to Louis Eliasberg Sr. A gem coin once owned by Jack Lee is one of two DMPL MS-65s.

1893-O
Certified Populations and Check List
Mint State

Circ	MS-60	MS-61	MS-62	MS-63	MS-64	MS-65	MS-66	MS-67	MS-68
2,658	63	139	360	306	85	6			

Prooflike

Circ	MS-60	MS-61	MS-62	MS-63	MS-64	MS-65	MS-66	MS-67	MS-68
	2	2	9	2			1		

Deep Mirror Prooflike

Circ	MS-60	MS-61	MS-62	MS-63	MS-64	MS-65	MS-66	MS-67	MS-68
			8	4		2			

1893-S

Mintage 100,000

Certified Population 4,926

Prooflike % 0.02

Deep Mirror Prooflike % 0.00

The 1895 Proof may be popularly referred to as the King of the Morgan Dollars, but it's more steward than heir to the throne. The true king is the Mint State 1893-S.

While most struck examples of the 1895 Proof survive in original Proof state, most of the 100,000 pieces struck by San Francisco in 1893 were either circulated or thrown into the smelter in 1918. Fewer than 100 Mint States examples are known.

Dealer John Love bought five coins out of a group of 28 Uncirculated examples discovered in an 1894-S Mint bag purchased from a Great Falls, Montana, bank in the early 1960s. Presumably the bag was packaged in early 1894, so it contained a handful of coins struck from the previous year's dies. Love believes that most extant Mint State pieces from this issue come from that same "hoard."

Another example handled by John was the Love-Rettew coin, sold in 1974.

In Mint State the 1893-S is a true rarity, and a major offering at any grade. A solitary MS-67 once belonging (at different times) to both Dr. Cornelius Vermeule and Jack Lee was the first Morgan dollar to sell in excess of $1 million.

In circulated grades the 1893-S runs the gamut, with prices exceeding $1,500 at Fair-2 and crossing the $5,000 threshold at Very Good. Of the 100,000 coins struck, fewer than 12,000 gradable coins are known. The 1893-S is a highly coveted 19th-century key-date coin.

For those pursuing a prooflike or deep mirror prooflike set, the 1893-S is the ultimate stopper. With only a handful of certified Mint State examples known, the probability that additional PL or DMPL coins will turn up is low. PCGS has deemed a single coin worthy of PL attribution, and that one earned a grade of only MS-62.

1893-S
Certified Populations and Chook List
Mint State

Circ	MS-60	MS-61	MS-62	MS-63	MS-64	MS-65	MS-66	MS-67	MS-68
4,889	2	9	6	9	4	5		1	

Prooflike

Circ	MS-60	MS-61	MS-62	MS-63	MS-64	MS-65	MS-66	MS-67	MS-68
			1						

Deep Mirror Prooflike

Circ	MS-60	MS-61	MS-62	MS-63	MS-64	MS-65	MS-66	MS-67	MS-68

1894

Mintage 110,000

Certified Population 4,301

Prooflike % 0.07

Deep Mirror Prooflike % 0.07

The 1894 is the lowest-produced Morgan dollar circulation strike issued by the Philadelphia Mint. For much of the series' history, however, this accolade belonged to the 1895, which reportedly had a mintage of 12,000 circulation strikes and 880 Proofs.

It turns out that was wrong. Apparently no circulation strikes were ever struck! It doesn't diminish the 1895 as a collector's coin, but if we are to be *numismatically* correct, the 1894 is the key-date Philly circulation strike in the Morgan dollar series.

The biggest infusion of these coins came in the late 1950s and early 1960s when the Treasury released a handful of bags into circulation. John Love remembers having a bag that he picked up in Great Falls, Montana.

At that time, the going rate per coin was $40 apiece in Uncirculated condition. Today the 1894 is well dispersed. Finding the date in roll quantity is highly unlikely, and most coin dealers don't keep the issue in stock.

Thanks to its scarcity, the 1894 Morgan dollar is collected in all grades. The coin sells for $500 in About Good and quickly climbs to $1,000 or more in Very Good. There is a slight upward lean in price through EF-40. In About Uncirculated, the coin starts to approach $2,000. Most of the surviving Mint State examples grade from MS-62 to MS-64. Gems are truly scarce, with 24 coins making the grade according to PCGS.

The 1894 is another stopper in prooflike and deep mirror prooflike. A mere six examples have been certified by PCGS: three MS-62 PLs, and one DMPL in each grade from MS-62 to MS-64.

1894
Certified Populations and Check List
Mint State

Circ	MS-60	MS-61	MS-62	MS-63	MS-64	MS-65	MS-66	MS-67	MS-68
3,102	54	176	365	331	243	20	4		

Prooflike

Circ	MS-60	MS-61	MS-62	MS-63	MS-64	MS-65	MS-66	MS-67	MS-68
			3						

Deep Mirror Prooflike

Circ	MS-60	MS-61	MS-62	MS-63	MS-64	MS-65	MS-66	MS-67	MS-68
			1	1	1				

Mintage 1,723,000

Certified Population. 4,647

Prooflike % 0.04

Deep Mirror Prooflike %. 0.06

In 1894, New Orleans led all three mints in Morgan dollar production. Demand for dollar coins was no stronger in 1894; the economic crisis that started in 1893 had only worsened through June. Growth would be lethargic for several years.

The New Orleans issue of 1894 is one of the least visually inspired Morgan dollars in the series. Most original Mint State coins are peach-colored or pale yellow, have lifeless surfaces, and feature no shortage of bag marks. Many well-struck examples have surface impediments that prevent them from grading above MS-64. A gem 1894-O is a true rarity.

Most Uncirculated examples on the market today were from bags released by the Trea-sury in the 1950s and 1960s. While this was a topsy-turvy period for the Morgan dollar market, the 1894-O was never available in plentiful numbers. In fact, the 1894-O is scarcer in Mint State than its mintage suggests.

PCGS's population reports indicate that in terms of the number of coins submitted for grading and authentication, the 1894-O is on par with the rare 1894-P, which has a total mintage 17 times lower!

Another 1890s Morgan dollar, another absolute stopper when it comes to Prooflike and Deep Mirror Prooflike examples. PCGS has certified two PLs (top pop grade being an MS-63), and three DMPLs (these being of even lower quality). Only the low end Mint State grades keep these expensive coins from achieving prices in excess of six figures.

1894-O
Certified Populations and Check List
Mint State

Circ	MS-60	MS-61	MS-62	MS-63	MS-64	MS-65	MS-66	MS-67	MS-68
3,470	66	184	298	303	310	11			

Prooflike

Circ	MS-60	MS-61	MS-62	MS-63	MS-64	MS-65	MS-66	MS-67	MS-68
		1		1					

Deep Mirror Prooflike

Circ	MS-60	MS-61	MS-62	MS-63	MS-64	MS-65	MS-66	MS-67	MS-68
		1	2						

1894-S

Mintage 1,260,000

Certified Population 4,450

Prooflike % 2.52

Deep Mirror Prooflike % 0.40

The most abundant 1894 Morgan dollar issue, in terms of survival rate, is the 1894-S. It is also better by a country mile in terms of strike quality in surfaces. The issue has nearly as many certified examples in MS-64 and above than either the 1894 or 1894-O have in Mint State, period. And while it may seem common relative to the two scarcer issues, the 1894-S was never available in abundance. The issue wasn't part of the Redfield hoard, which featured a large contingent of other San Francisco coinage.

When the Treasury released bags from this issue, it was done in isolated pockets of the country. Of one release in Montana, John Love remembers most being bag marked but typically brilliant.

The days of finding most dates in Mint-sewn bags are long since past. Love sees a handful of 1894-S's cycle through each month; many are Uncirculated or in the lower Mint State grades. Gems are scarce but do trade a couple of times a year, usually at major auctions.

For those putting together a date set of prooflike or deep mirror prooflike Morgan dollars, the 1894-S is likely your only chance, as time and attrition have left us with only a handful of examples from the other mints. Having said that, the 1894-S is rare in DMPL. In prooflike, the issue is scarce, with only two coins grading MS-65.

1894-S
Certified Populations and Check List
Mint State

Circ	MS-60	MS-61	MS-62	MS-63	MS-64	MS-65	MS-66	MS-67	MS-68
1,210	70	253	730	1,074	829	142	10	2	

Prooflike

Circ	MS-60	MS-61	MS-62	MS-63	MS-64	MS-65	MS-66	MS-67	MS-68
	9	16	27	30	28	2			

Deep Mirror Prooflike

Circ	MS-60	MS-61	MS-62	MS-63	MS-64	MS-65	MS-66	MS-67	MS-68
	1	1	6	8	2				

1895 (Proof)

Mintage 880

Certified Population. 505

Cameo % 15.64

Deep Cameo % 3.76

For much of the last century, numismatists sought out any one of 12,000 1895 Morgan dollars allegedly struck by the Philadelphia Mint. Indeed, the coins were on their books, and the Mint went so far as to list the number of dies prepared for coining. But no examples were known to have been released in the 19th century, and no supposed example passed the scrutiny of authentication in the 20th. What happened was a wild-goose chase, more than 100 years long, for an issue of which circulation strikes were most likely never made.

The fact that no one ever could confirm its existence didn't stop coin doctors and counterfeiters. The skillful removal of an O or S mintmark was the origin of many a fake. Others were cast forgeries. Today, foreign counterfeiters ap-ply their trade to fool consumers into believing that they've stumbled upon one of the 19th century's key rarities.

The King of the Morgan Dollars, it seems, is a Proof-only issue.

At 880 coins struck, the 1895 isn't even the scarcest of the Morgan Proof issues. The 1884-P has a mintage of 875 and routinely sells for a few thousand dollars. Ten dates have Proof mintages under 800, including the 1890 (which boasts only 590). Still, the lack of a circulation strike out of Philadelphia in 1895 makes this not-intended-for-circulation coin essential for completionists.

As is the case with most "classic-era" Proofs, the quality of the coin today depends largely on its state of preservation. 1895 Proofs were beautifully struck, and several have cameo characteristics. Deep cameos are rare. PCGS has graded one PF-68DCAM—a grade more commonly attributed to modern-day releases, not ultra-rare 19th-century classics.

1895, Proof
Certified Populations and Check List

Proof

Impaired	PF-60	PF-61	PF-62	PF-63	PF-64	PF-65	PF-66	PF-67	PF-68
104	15	38	86	72	56	14	16	5	1

Cameo

Impaired	PF-60	PF-61	PF-62	PF-63	PF-64	PF-65	PF-66	PF-67	PF-68
		2	12	18	25	13	3	6	

Deep Cameo

Circ	PF-60	PF-61	PF-62	PF-63	PF-64	PF-65	PF-66	PF-67	PF-68
				1	3	4	6	4	1

1895-O

Mintage 450,000

Certified Population. 5,287

Prooflike % 0.08

Deep Mirror Prooflike %. 0.13

The mid-decade decline in Morgan dollar production wasn't unexpected following legislation that stopped the government from purchasing millions of dollars, worth of silver bullion every month. Without it, and without any dispersal from the Treasury's vaults, natural demand for the coin would have spurred production of a million or so coins per mint—but the Panic of 1893 had all but depleted the need for additional silver-dollar coinage.

1895 marks the first year when only branch mints produced Morgan dollars for circulation. Of the two branches, New Orleans produced the most, outpacing San Francisco by 50,000 pieces. Unfortunately for collectors, this advantage doesn't play out in the number of Mint

State survivors: the 1895-O is the third-rarest Morgan dollar in Uncirculated condition. Only Mint State examples of the 1892-S and 1893-S are rarer.

Most collectors will have to be content owning a circulated example from this issue. It's offered regularly in all circulated grades. In About Uncirculated, the coin finds a market filled with eager buyers.

Uncirculated coins number in the low hundreds, with the heaviest concentration falling in the MS-61 to MS-63 range. PCGS has graded eight gems, including the condition-census piece, an MS-67 once belonging to Wayne Miller and Jack Lee.

In prooflike and deep mirror prooflike, the issue is rarer than Massachusetts Bay silver coinage. Only 11 pieces have been certified as such by PCGS, the highest-graded example being a lightly toned gem MS-65DMPL. It is also formerly part of the Jack Lee collection.

1895-O
Certified Populations and Check List
Mint State

Circ	MS-60	MS-61	MS-62	MS-63	MS-64	MS-65	MS-66	MS-67	MS-68
5,145	21	32	41	19	11	5	1	1	

Prooflike

Circ	MS-60	MS-61	MS-62	MS-63	MS-64	MS-65	MS-66	MS-67	MS-68
		1		2	1				

Deep Mirror Prooflike

Circ	MS-60	MS-61	MS-62	MS-63	MS-64	MS-65	MS-66	MS-67	MS-68
	1	2	3			1			

1895-S

Mintage	400,000
Certified Population	3,622
Prooflike %	2.24
Deep Mirror Prooflike %	1.10

With a mintage 50,000 coins lower than the 1895-O, the 1895-S has experienced a better survival rate than its Cajun cousin, and because of this it is priced well below the 1895-O and the Proof-only 1895-P. Nevertheless, the 1895-S is one of the toughest dates in the series.

It's also one of the great 19th-century issues.

In terms of aesthetics, the 1895-S is frustrating. While the coin features a consistently good strike and excellent luster, it is one of the least attractive Morgan dollars struck by the San Francisco Mint. The reason? Surface abrasion.

Unsightly bag marks are at their most prevalent with the 1895-S. The issue provides few truly attractive coins. Because of this issue,

out of the 1,200+ Mint State coins PCGS has certified since 1985, just 41 have graded gem or better.

About 1,000 pieces were discovered in the Redfield hoard. While nearly all of them are heavily bag marked, beware of non-certified examples with counting-wheel marks. These will most likely earn a details grade from a reputable service.

The grade with the largest variance in eye appeal is MS-64. Collectors who prefer brilliant coins will have to assess their tolerance for marks on Liberty's face, while those who prefer toned coinage may find some attractive examples whose toning conceals otherwise visible flaws.

Collectors buying circulated pieces benefit from lower prices.

For prooflike and deep mirror prooflike collectors, the 1895-S offers some relief relative to the 1895-O.

1895-S
Certified Populations and Check List
Mint State

Circ	MS-60	MS-61	MS-62	MS-63	MS-64	MS-65	MS-66	MS-67	MS-68
2,358	27	112	228	356	383	35	2		

Prooflike

Circ	MS-60	MS-61	MS-62	MS-63	MS-64	MS-65	MS-66	MS-67	MS-68
	7	10	24	23	16	1			

Deep Mirror Prooflike

Circ	MS-60	MS-61	MS-62	MS-63	MS-64	MS-65	MS-66	MS-67	MS-68
	1	2	7	6	21		2	1	

1896

Mintage 9,976,000

Certified Population. 36,388

Prooflike % 2.40

Deep Mirror Prooflike %. 1.99

When the Bland-Allison Act was signed into law in 1878, the total coinage and bullion of the United States amounted to about $135 million in gold and $6.15 million in silver. Uncovered paper accounted for nearly $750 million of the monetary supply, the highest amount of any of the major nations in the 19th century.[25]

When the Panic of 1893 hit, the amount of silver coinage produced by the United States had surpassed gold due to the extraction of gold from the economy. The repeal of the Sherman Silver Purchase Act, and the government's efforts to reinforce its position in gold, gave the two metals parity in the American economy. On paper, there was balance. In reality, silver sat in government stockpiles, worth a little more than 60 percent of its face value.

So in 1896, Morgan dollar production returned to its pre-1892 levels. Led by Philadel-phia's robust output, a total of 19,876,000 coins were struck.

In the Morgan dollar series, there's usually a correlation between high mintages and low-quality coins. This is less true for San Francisco's share (perhaps because it was the most technologically advanced mint in the United States), but it's definitely true looking at the year's production from Philadelphia and New Orleans. Yet the 1896 Philly strike is a wonderful exception to this rule and is one of the Mother Mint's best efforts in the entire series.

Ample amounts of original Uncirculated material survive, so the 1896 is readily available in grades MS-62 through MS-65, with plenty of MS-66s should you want to stretch your budget and own one of the better-looking Morgan dollars in the series. Strike typically shows full details, surfaces are frosty, and the coins can exhibit great luster. One almost expects an S mintmark on the reverse, the quality is so good.

Prooflike and deep cameo prooflike examples are readily available all the way up to MS-65.

1896
Certified Populations and Check List

Mint State

Circ	MS-60	MS-61	MS-62	MS-63	MS-64	MS-65	MS-66	MS-67	MS-68
829	53	419	3,679	12,470	12,895	3,667	737	40	

Prooflike

Circ	MS-60	MS-61	MS-62	MS-63	MS-64	MS-65	MS-66	MS-67	MS-68
	3	16	133	303	310	94	14	1	

Deep Mirror Prooflike

Circ	MS-60	MS-61	MS-62	MS-63	MS-64	MS-65	MS-66	MS-67	MS-68
	6	23	83	219	249	130	14	1	

1896-O

Mintage	4,900,000
Certified Population	5,167
Prooflike %	0.15
Deep Mirror Prooflike %	0.29

Despite the fact that several Mint-sewn bags of 1896-O Morgan dollars were released in the 1950s and 1960s by the Treasury Department, the coin is not widely available in Mint State. One wonders, given the quality of the Uncirculated coins that represent this date, whether these bags contained any gems at all. If they did, then clearly the market price over the past 20 years would have been high enough to bring them out.

The 1896-O is an excellent case study in the value collectors place on conditional rarity. The coin is scarce in Mint State, but it's absolutely rare in grades above MS-64. To date, PCGS has graded three gems: one in MS-65 and two in MS-66. The MS-66 examples have sold for twice the amount of the sole 65, more than 60 times that of an MS-63, and 400 times the price of an MS-60! That's quite a premium to pay for the aesthetics of a coin. But it's where the market is today.

It's hard to single out what holds this issue back in terms of quality. If you wanted to teach a master's class on how not to make a coin, the 1896-O would be exhibits A, B, and C. Most Mint State examples do away with any pretense of luster or strike. Those few that have excellent luster and strike (through no fault of the coiners!) invariably fall victim to surface abrasions and bag marks.

Miraculously, at least three true gems are out there. How many more are there? We may never know.

Prooflike and deep mirror prooflike 1896-O dollars are impossibly rare.

A Coin of Dubious Origin: Since at least the 1960s, but possibly even earlier than that, an imposter 1896-O circulated bearing a "micro O" mintmark. The counterfeit fooled even professional numismatists for generations until PCGS compared examples to several other curious Micro O Morgans. It turns out that *all* Micro O Morgans from 1896, 1900, and 1902 are fakes! The spurious coins all share the same reverse (virtually impossible given the spread of dates), along with a number of other characteristics. Most of the impostor 1896-Os were circulated.

1896-O
Certified Populations and Check List
Mint State

Circ	MS-60	MS-61	MS-62	MS-63	MS-64	MS-65	MS-66	MS-67	MS-68
3,841	114	324	552	284	26	1	2		

Prooflike

Circ	MS-60	MS-61	MS-62	MS-63	MS-64	MS-65	MS-66	MS-67	MS-68
	4	1	3						

Deep Mirror Prooflike

Circ	MS-60	MS-61	MS-62	MS-63	MS-64	MS-65	MS-66	MS-67	MS-68
	1	2	3						

1896-S

Mintage 5,000,000

Certified Population 2,623

Prooflike % 0.27

Deep Mirror Prooflike % 0.00

A number of 1896-S Morgan dollars circulated in the 19th and early-20th centuries, as evidenced by how relatively easy it is to find a well-worn example. The closer it is to Mint State, the tougher it is to procure. The current market bears prices approaching $1,000 for About Uncirculated examples, as collectors stretch their budgets to get the next-best thing.

It's assumed that most of the issue was lost due to the Pittman Act. A bag or two might have been released in the 1950s, because the supply was just large enough to keep the coin from being considered a major rarity.

This quickly changed, however, as silver dollars became the most important niche in American coin collecting starting in the 1960s.

In 1960, the 1896-S sold for $20 to $25 in Mint State.[26] By 1974, the last year the *Coin Dealer Newsletter* listed Morgan dollars simply as Uncs, the price had risen to $415 dealer ask.[27]

Collectors were treated to several hundred new-to-the-market pieces when the contents of the Redfield hoard became known. John Love recounts that the hoard contained a few hundred coins in Mint State. These exhibited solid strikes but were heavily bag marked. Most of the coins on the market today are from the Redfield hoard and, based on PCGS population report, we can assume that most of the Redfield 1896-S's graded from MS-62 to MS-64.

Assembling a complete set of 1890s Morgan dollars in prooflike would accomplish one of the more difficult challenges in American numismatics. The 1896-S has yielded few prooflike examples and no deep mirror prooflikes.

1896-S
Certified Populations and Check List
Mint State

Circ	MS-60	MS-61	MS-62	MS-63	MS-64	MS-65	MS-66	MS-67	MS-68
1,101	26	123	368	506	427	62	2	1	

Prooflike

Circ	MS-60	MS-61	MS-62	MS-63	MS-64	MS-65	MS-66	MS-67	MS-68
	1		1	3		1	1		

Deep Mirror Prooflike

Circ	MS-60	MS-61	MS-62	MS-63	MS-64	MS-65	MS-66	MS-67	MS-68

1897

Mintage	2,822,000
Certified Population.	14,766
Prooflike %	3.21
Deep Mirror Prooflike %.	1.43

Overall, dollar production in 1897 was off from 1896, when the coin re-emerged after five years on life-support. The Philadelphia Mint struck Morgan dollars sporadically throughout the year. The bulk of the date's 2.8 million mintage was struck during three months: January, June, and December. An overwhelming majority of the issue was put away in storage until the dollars were melted and sold as bullion to the British in 1918.

Because of this, the issue eluded collectors for many years until significant numbers of bags entered circulation in the 1950s and 1960s. By the end of the great silver-dollar rush of the 1960s, the 1897 issue was plentiful. Dozens of additional bags came to light in the mid-1970s when A-Mark purchased the Redfield hoard.

To the uninitiated, the issue's low mintage camouflaged its ready availability, and many unassuming investors and inexperienced collectors in the late 1970s and early 1980s fell for the pitch that this was a scarce date or a potential "sleeper coin."

The term *sleeper* might be a stretch when describing the 1897 Philly strike, as much of the issue's numismatic premium in grades through MS-63 is based in the appeal of owning an Uncirculated U.S. coin that's more than 110 years old.

But the market for the coin does pick up at MS-65 and beyond. It's at this grade and higher that the funnel of available coins for serious collectors begins to narrow. The 1897 will never be a tough issue compared to any of the scarcer 1890s issues, but the coin still presents a challenge for those who desire to have the very best coins.

Prooflike and deep mirror prooflike collectors will have an easier time with this release than with most 1890s issues. It's more common to find examples with deeply mirrored fields than highly contrasting cameos.

1897
Certified Populations and Check List
Mint State

Circ	MS-60	MS-61	MS-62	MS-63	MS-64	MS-65	MS-66	MS-67	MS-68
526	28	186	1,389	5,069	5,088	1,486	292	17	

Prooflike

Circ	MS-60	MS-61	MS-62	MS-63	MS-64	MS-65	MS-66	MS-67	MS-68
	5	18	87	155	157	43	9		

Deep Mirror Prooflike

Circ	MS-60	MS-61	MS-62	MS-63	MS-64	MS-65	MS-66	MS-67	MS-68
		12	32	68	71	26	2		

1897-O

Mintage 4,004,000

Certified Population 5,426

Prooflike % 0.20

Deep Mirror Prooflike % 0.22

The New Orleans Mint put out a workmanlike quantity of four million Morgan dollars in 1897, good enough to nearly split the difference between the output of San Francisco and Philadelphia. A sizeable but unknown amount of the issue circulated in the 19th and early-20th centuries, but it's assumed that most of the mintage was melted. A few bags of Uncirculated coins (as well as some sliders) found their way into the coin market in the 1950s and 1960s, but these bags were not nearly enough to supply the modern Morgan dollar collector market.

In terms of collecting, the 1897-O was a bit of a controversial coin. In the early 1980s many dealers felt that the 1897-O had become overrated as a conditional rarity. Some chafed at the idea that the issue was comparable to the New Orleans issue of a year before, as some coin promoters intimated. Steve Ivy and Ron Howard said as much in their 1984 book, *What Every Silver Dollar Buyer Should Know*, writing that the 1897-O was "significantly more common than the 1896-O."[28] Well, after nearly 30 years of grading Morgan dollars, the results are in: the 1897-O is four times as common as the 1896-O. The thing is, there were only three gems certified by PCGS for that year and a mere twelve for this issue. So we're not exactly talking apples and oranges in terms of scarcity. They both are tough dates.

For collectors in the market for circulated coinage of this release, the 1897-O is readily available in grades through AU-58. The issue starts to acquire a numismatic premium at EF-45.

A coin that is scarce in Mint State is typically going to be scarce in prooflike and deep mirror prooflike and the 1897-O is no exception. Whatever Uncirculated bags survived long enough for the market to take stock in such things contained only a handful of frosty cameo coins or pieces with deep reflective mirrors. The 1897-O isn't the toughest New Orleans issue for these categorizations, but it's pretty close.

1897-O
Certified Populations and Check List
Mint State

Circ	MS-60	MS-61	MS-62	MS-63	MS-64	MS-65	MS-66	MS-67	MS-68
3,498	725	335	557	246	30	6	4	2	

Prooflike

Circ	MS-60	MS-61	MS-62	MS-63	MS-64	MS-65	MS-66	MS-67	MS-68
	1	2	4	4					

Deep Mirror Prooflike

Circ	MS-60	MS-61	MS-62	MS-63	MS-64	MS-65	MS-66	MS-67	MS-68
	2	2	6		2				

1897-S

Mintage 5,825,000

Certified Population. 10,043

Prooflike % 8.95

Deep Mirror Prooflike %. 2.08

As a class, the 1897-S Morgan dollar is the best-struck, most attractive coin of its year of issue. Most coins as struck have clear details, frosty lustrous surfaces, and great eye appeal. While bag marks from mishandling over the years put a limit on the number of pristine examples that survive, by and large, collectors should have no problem acquiring an example that suits their tastes.

A number of bags were released in the 19th and early-20th centuries, when the coins circulated as a routine part of everyday commerce. This accounts for the commonality of the issue in circulated grades. In Mint State, much of what exists in the market comes from bags released by the Treasury over the course of many years, culminating with the great silver release of the 1960s.

It was from these releases that LaVere Redfield accumulated his holdings of the issue. By some accounts, the Redfield hoard contained 20,000 to 25,000 Mint State examples, many with significant bag marks. The quantity of coins took several years for A-Mark and its distributors to sell through, but once the issue had been dispersed, the price of the coins began to increase (though only slightly).

As grading for the coin grew more sophisticated, so too did the appreciation of exceptional examples of all Morgan dollars. The 1897-S is reasonably priced through MS-64, as it is most common in these grades, but at MS-65 and above, availability quickly begins to taper off. Collectors desiring the very best have to deal with the competition of similarly focused individuals.

In prooflike, the 1897-S is one of the more plentiful issues of the 1890s. This isn't the case for deep mirror prooflikes, which are significantly more difficult to find but are by no means rare until in grades less than gem. One superlative example, the top-pop MS-67DMPL, is a beautiful coin with deep fields and creamy frosty-white devices. The coin reminds one of Miss Liberty aloft on a calm black duck pond. Simply exquisite.

1897-S
Certified Populations and Check List
Mint State

Circ	MS-60	MS-61	MS-62	MS-63	MS-64	MS-65	MS-66	MS-67	MS-68
589	32	186	1,061	2,849	2,888	1,071	237	20	2

Prooflike

Circ	MS-60	MS-61	MS-62	MS-63	MS-64	MS-65	MS-66	MS-67	MS-68
	5	28	112	303	295	131	23	2	

Deep Mirror Prooflike

Circ	MS-60	MS-61	MS-62	MS-63	MS-64	MS-65	MS-66	MS-67	MS-68
	3	5	26	55	80	33	6	1	

1898

Mintage 5,884,000

Certified Population. 17,117

Prooflike % 4.24

Deep Mirror Prooflike %. 2.30

You could make the argument that the 1898 is perhaps the best-quality Philly-strike issue of the Morgan dollar series. Beautiful well-struck pieces abound, while truly exceptional pieces have dazzling highly lustrous surfaces and fully transferred design elements that are just hammered onto the planchet. If only every Morgan dollar could look like this, right?

A majority of the coins that survive from this issue were released in the 1950s and 1960s. Still more turned up in the LaVere Redfield hoard (perhaps as many as 15,000 pieces). John Love recalls a majority of these going to hard-money advocate John Kamin.

The typical Uncirculated 1898 grades from MS-62 to MS-64, but gems are plentiful. For coinage that is more than 100 years old and was stacked indiscriminately in 60-pound cloth sacks, you couldn't ask for better. As is the case with any coin available in quantity, be selective about strike, color, luster, and surfaces. There's plenty of material here to allow you to get what you want.

Obtaining a prooflike or deep mirror prooflike example from this date should require little effort. While not as plentiful as the 1898-O, a sufficient number of examples exist to satisfy the current demands of the marketplace. The expected grade of coins with DMPL or PL attribution will mirror the general population of brilliant Uncirculated pieces.

1898
Certified Populations and Check List
Mint State

Circ	MS-60	MS-61	MS-62	MS-63	MS-64	MS-65	MS-66	MS-67	MS-68
545	34	166	1,426	5,174	5,862	2,149	600	42	

Prooflike

Circ	MS-60	MS-61	MS-62	MS-63	MS-64	MS-65	MS-66	MS-67	MS-68
	6	16	110	217	260	106	11		

Deep Mirror Prooflike

Circ	MS-60	MS-61	MS-62	MS-63	MS-64	MS-65	MS-66	MS-67	MS-68
	4	13	47	114	144	58	12	1	

1898-O

Mintage 4,440,000

Certified Population 61,263

Prooflike % 1.84

Deep Mirror Prooflike % 1.25

The 1898-O is a legendary coin in terms of the issue's reversal of fortune on the numismatic marketplace. Despite the fact that 4.4 million pieces were struck this year by the New Orleans Mint, most numismatists never saw one. Many assumed that the bulk of the mintage had been melted and the few coins that survived were highly prized—*if* you could get your hands on one.

If you had the means and could find an 1898-O Morgan dollar in 1962, when the issue was at its peak in rarity and price, the coin would have set you back $300. That's $2,314 in today's money when adjusted for inflation.

The closest the issue came to achieving that price was at the height of a strong Morgan dollar market in 1986, when an MS-65 example commanded $615. When adjusted for inflation, that total comes out to be $1,331, a little more than half its prior high. In today's market you can split the difference and take home one of the more than 160 superb gem MS-67 examples that have been graded by PCGS.

The precipitous decline in the value of the 1898-O, along with its O-Mint siblings of 1903 and 1904, illustrate just how much numismatists of the period didn't know about the Morgan dollar series, as the modern marketplace for the coin was beginning to form. Dealers and collectors understood which pieces were difficult to obtain, but nobody was fully aware of the extent that the government's stockpile of dollar coins could radically alter the market. Dates that the government didn't have almost all became winners, and issues like this one, which were available by the hundreds of thousands, became the series' losers.

The exact total of 1898-O dollars released in late 1962 is anybody's guess. But judging by the fact that the coin was trading at $4 apiece in 1970, that number must have been high, perhaps 100,000 to 1 million pieces. Today the 1898-O is one of the more common New Orleans issues and is certainly one of the nicest. The typical Uncirculated example will fall in the MS-63 to MS-65 grade range.

In prooflike and deep mirror prooflike, the 1898-O is widely available. The finest certified example of the entire issue is a remarkable MS-68DMPL that was formerly owned by Jack Lee.

1898-O
Certified Populations and Check List
Mint State

Circ	MS-60	MS-61	MS-62	MS-63	MS-64	MS-65	MS-66	MS-67	MS-68
54	33	184	2,104	16,209	27,525	11,225	1,870	161	

Prooflike

Circ	MS-60	MS-61	MS-62	MS-63	MS-64	MS-65	MS-66	MS-67	MS-68
	3	13	95	357	410	201	50	1	

Deep Mirror Prooflike

Circ	MS-60	MS-61	MS-62	MS-63	MS-64	MS-65	MS-66	MS-67	MS-68
	2	12	65	185	309	152	40	2	1

1898-S

Mintage 4,102,000

Certified Population 4,639

Prooflike % 3.13

Deep Mirror Prooflike % 1.81

Throughout the first 60 or so years of the 20th century, the 1898-S, with its mintage of 4.1 million coins, traded as a common-date Morgan dollar. Few collectors, and the widespread release of the issue at the end of World War I (and then again after World War II), meant that supply was ample. Small caches of the coin were saved beyond what was needed by the numismatic market at the time. What wasn't needed remained in circulation.

Few bags of 1898-S dollars were released in the 1960s when interest in the Morgan dollar series was picking up steam. A few hundred examples did turn up in the Redfield hoard, but this accumulation was hardly enough to redefine the issue's scarcity level.

One of the frustrating features of the 1898-S, which makes it in some respects similar

to the 1879-O, is that a large number of coins from the issue are poorly struck. On poorly struck examples, even Mint State coins can look lightly circulated. To add to the confusion, a large number of About Uncirculated coins exist from this issue. Graders and collectors have to carefully scrutinize the surfaces to ensure accurate grading.

In Mint State, the typical 1898-S example grades from MS-62 to MS-64. Many coins will be limited by either bag marks or quality of strike. Gems are not common and anything above MS-65 is scarce. Well-struck examples with minimal marks are premium coins for this issue and will likely command more money at auction. A sole example sits at MS-68, a semi-prooflike piece with soft lilac toning that once belonged in Jack Lee's fantastic collection of Morgan dollars.

Although there are many coins that exhibit prooflike tendencies, prooflike and deep mirror prooflike coins are scarce for the 1898-S. To date, PCGS has not graded a single one above MS-65.

1898-S
Certified Populations and Check List
Mint State

Circ	MS-60	MS-61	MS-62	MS-63	MS-64	MS-65	MS-66	MS-67	MS-68
963	36	146	532	1,096	1,167	402	65	2	1

Prooflike

Circ	MS-60	MS-61	MS-62	MS-63	MS-64	MS-65	MS-66	MS-67	MS-68
	3	11	38	54	34	5			

Deep Mirror Prooflike

Circ	MS-60	MS-61	MS-62	MS-63	MS-64	MS-65	MS-66	MS-67	MS-68
		2	9	32	34	7			

Mintage	330,886
Certified Population	11,989
Prooflike %	3.19
Deep Mirror Prooflike %	2.00

It's doubtful that very many 1899 Morgan dollars circulated, simply because the coin was seldom seen before a rush of them was released decades later across the country. By some estimates as much as two-thirds of Philadelphia's 330,000-coin output sat in storage until the middle of the 20th century.

To the uninitiated, this issue's low mintage would be reason enough to stock up on the date—and in the investment boom period of the 1970s and 1980s, this is exactly what happened as stacks of 1899s entered into investors' portfolios at peak prices. Some tried to discredit this practice by questioning the issue's mintage total, implying that perhaps millions were made. With the number of Uncirculated pieces that flooded the market it might have seemed that way, but it wasn't true. The Philadelphia Mint struggled all year to keep up with its primary mission to supply the nation with coinage. Morgan dollar production was ancillary to that goal, which is obvious when you consider how few went into the streams of commerce.

The 1899 has a dubious history as a collectible coin as it was a favorite of promoters who sold untold thousands of the date at inflated prices. Investors dreaming of big returns had only the issue's low mintage to guide them into the irrational decision to hoard the coins at top-of-the-market prices. They didn't realize so many of them were floating around wholesale channels.

Today the 1899 is fairly well dispersed. The days of the coin being over-promoted are likely over for good. The issue remains popular and may even prove to be a sleeper, depending on how much the Morgan dollar market grows in the coming years. In terms of market price, it's firmly distanced itself from the more common dates and is seen in the same light as the 1883 or 1884 Carson City issues.

The quality of this issue runs the gamut, but like the 1898, which provided collectors with some exceptional coins, the 1899 is similarly good, maybe a half step below. The average Uncirculated example will likely fall into the MS-62 to MS-64 range. Gems aren't as common, but are by no means scarce. A number of exceptional superb gems have been graded by PCGS to date.

While the issue typically has frosty luster, semi-prooflike examples are occasionally seen. True prooflike and deep mirror prooflike examples are uncommon. In today's market prooflikes bring about double the price of the typical Uncirculated piece in most grades. Deep mirror prooflikes can bring up to three times as much.

1899
Certified Populations and Check List

Mint State

Circ	MS-60	MS-61	MS-62	MS-63	MS-64	MS-65	MS-66	MS-67	MS-68
1,137	39	238	1,336	3,587	3,710	1,101	200	18	

Prooflike

Circ	MS-60	MS-61	MS-62	MS-63	MS-64	MS-65	MS-66	MS-67	MS-68
	3	8	40	102	149	74	7		

Deep Mirror Prooflike

Circ	MS-60	MS-61	MS-62	MS-63	MS-64	MS-65	MS-66	MS-67	MS-68
	1	4	27	64	85	48	11		

1899-O

Mintage 12,290,000

Certified Population. 50,849

Prooflike % 0.43

Deep Mirror Prooflike %. 0.43

The task of minting the bulk of 1899's silver dollars fell to the New Orleans Mint, which struck 12.29 million coins, eclipsing their previous high total of 12.15 million, set in 1888. A small portion of the overall mintage circulated at the time they were struck; the rest were holed up in government vaults. The coins that survived the Pittman Act—a significant amount, but likely no more than a million coins—were released into circulation after World War II, culminating with the major New Orleans release in late 1962. Today the coin is as plentiful as any pre-1921 Morgan dollar.

While the quality of the issue varies in large part due to die state and the number of surface abrasions, enough 1899-O dollars survive that collectors have the ability to select a coin that fits their aesthetic needs. Well-struck examples with robust luster are not uncommon for this release.

The typical Uncirculated 1899-O will fall in the grading range of MS-62 to MS-64. Gems are not tough to come by, but naturally aren't as plentiful as examples in the choice grade range. Jack Lee's MS-68 is the standard bearer for the issue. It features an above-average strike with almost flawless surfaces.

Of the three 1899 issues, the 1899-O is in the middle in terms of scarcity of prooflike and deep mirror prooflike coins. Surface abrasions and eye appeal are the key detriments for those earning high grades. Two spectacular examples have graded MS-67DMPL.

Micro-O and the Micro-Faux: The 1899 New Orleans issue has a highly sought-after collectible variety known as the 1899-O, Micro O. The variety is called this because it contains a

Barber quarter mintmark that was mistakenly used on at least five 1899 reverse dies. The variety was discovered in 1951 and was a sensation amongst Morgan dollar variety collectors, especially after the publication of Leroy Van Allen and A. George Mallis's landmark work on the subject in the 1950s and 1960s. Today, few examples are known in Mint State, while a thousand or more examples have been found in the circulated grades.

The popularity of the Micro O variety led to some unscrupulous coin doctors to ply their trade on unsuspecting collectors by manufacturing Micro O's for 1896, 1900, and 1902. It wasn't until 2005 that PCGS's expert variety specialists reviewed a collection of high-grade examples, revealing that all three of these dates were phony! The chicanery was uncovered because all three dates featured the exact same reverse die. It's well known that New Orleans liked to extend the life of their dies, but it's not conceivable to think that one die would be used over the course of six years!

1899-O
Certified Populations and Check List
Mint State

Circ	MS-60	MS-61	MS-62	MS-63	MS-64	MS-65	MS-66	MS-67	MS-68
257	41	263	2,995	16,872	21,375	7,286	1,221	97	1

Prooflike

Circ	MS-60	MS-61	MS-62	MS-63	MS-64	MS-65	MS-66	MS-67	MS-68
	1	8	23	63	75	38	13		

Deep Mirror Prooflike

Circ	MS-60	MS-61	MS-62	MS-63	MS-64	MS-65	MS-66	MS-67	MS-68
	1	3	19	52	80	44	19	2	

1899-S

Mintage 2,562,000

Certified Population. 4,639

Prooflike % 3.13

Deep Mirror Prooflike %. 1.81

In 1899, the San Francisco Mint struck Morgan dollars from January through July. Its output of 2.56 million coins, by and large, went directly into storage. In circulated grades the 1899-S is very scarce. The coin was also scarce in Uncirculated grades until the end of World War II. In the 1940s and 1950s what remained of its mintage dribbled out. Dealers acquired a number of bags and had little problem supplying collectors of that era with coins. The mid-century Morgan dollar collector base was small and there was no sense that the coin was particularly rare.

The 1899-S traded for about $4.50 in Uncirculated condition in 1960.[29] When the coin didn't show up in subsequent Treasury releases, opinions about the issue changed. By 1965, Uncirculated examples were trading around $50. By 1980, the price had risen above $400. When the industry adopted the 11-point Mint State grading system in 1986, collectors and investors focused on the very best examples and the prices of premium Morgan dollars reached peaks unheard-of just a few years before.

For its part, the 1899-S has always been modestly priced in the upper echelons, in large part due to the fact that overall this is a well-made issue. The typical Uncirculated 1899-S dollar will fall between the grades MS-62 and MS-64. Most of these are beautifully struck coins, which are graded according to the degree of bag marks that are present. Several hundred gem-quality coins are known and 10 superb gems round up the top of the population chart.

Being that the 1899-S is a scarce issue to begin with, proof-like examples of the 1899-S are well represented in grades MS-63 through MS-65. In deep mirror prooflike, the coin becomes much more scarce. When a majority of the coins from this issue were saved, almost no regard was paid to mirror-like finishes or cameo contrast, so one can only imagine how many truly spectacular examples there might still be out there.

1899-S
Certified Populations and Check List
Mint State

Circ	MS-60	MS-61	MS-62	MS-63	MS-64	MS-65	MS-66	MS-67	MS-68
606	34	108	469	1,134	1,277	412	109	8	

Prooflike

Circ	MS-60	MS-61	MS-62	MS-63	MS-64	MS-65	MS-66	MS-67	MS-68
	1	8	18	51	69	38	2	2	

Deep Mirror Prooflike

Circ	MS-60	MS-61	MS-62	MS-63	MS-64	MS-65	MS-66	MS-67	MS-68
		1	5	11	23	2	4		

Mintage	8,830,000
Certified Population	29,880
Prooflike %	0.25
Deep Mirror Prooflike %	0.01

The last year of the 19th century saw the Morgan dollar resurgent, as the combined mintage from all three facilities topped 20 million pieces for the first time since 1891 (the height of the Sherman Silver Purchase Act). The year also saw the introduction of a new reverse hub. Van Allen and Mallis refer to the new hub as C4.

Completionists tend to seek out one of each, but mainstream collectors are usually satisfied with one attractive and well-struck 1900 Morgan dollar. As a numismatic exercise, however, it is interesting to compare two almost indiscernible hub varieties side-by-side.

In terms of what to expect, the 1900 is a mixed bag. Yes, the coin has strong representation in MS-65 and MS-66, but an overwhelming majority of coins from this issue have strikes best described as mediocre. The lack of representation on the lower end of the Mint State scale in the population chart below is more indicative of the quality of coins submitted for encapsulation than of the quality of coins as they exist in the wild.

Through the 1970s and 1980s, the 1900 was traded like a bullion coin or a common silver dollar. This changed when the coin was more widely dispersed and original bags dried up. Today it's ripe for cherrypicking, especially when it comes to attractive well-struck coins with minimal bag marks. The market for these coins has nowhere to go but up.

This is an issue that's scarce in prooflike and rare in deep mirror prooflike. In PL the coin falls between the grades MS-62 and MS-66, with the heaviest concentration in the 63–65 range. PCGS has certified four DMPLs. In 2008 Heritage sold one of two top-pop MS-65 DMPLs for a staggering $51,750.[30]

1900
Certified Populations and Check List
Mint State

Circ	MS-60	MS-61	MS-62	MS-63	MS-64	MS-65	MS-66	MS-67	MS-68
592	47	147	1,806	9,686	13,366	3,557	575	25	

Prooflike

Circ	MS-60	MS-61	MS-62	MS-63	MS-64	MS-65	MS-66	MS-67	MS-68
			5	16	27	22	5		

Deep Mirror Prooflike

Circ	MS-60	MS-61	MS-62	MS-63	MS-64	MS-65	MS-66	MS-67	MS-68
					2	2			

1900-O

Mintage 12,590,000

Certified Population......... 37,619

Prooflike % 1.12

Deep Mirror Prooflike %..... 0.09

In 1900 New Orleans ramped up Morgan dollar production by 300,000 coins, striking 12.59 million pieces. Production peaked in the first six months of the year, with an average of 1.5 million coins per month. The only month the dollar wasn't struck was October.

As the issue was struck in such volume, the quality of individual coins depends heavily on die state, striking pressure, and the care with which the coin was handled. The issue was never scarce, even before the Treasury opened its vaults and untold hundreds of thousands of 1900-P's came onto the market in the 1960s.

Solid coins with solid strikes offer collectors the best way to enjoy this issue. Expect the typical Mint State 1900-O to grade from MS-62 to MS-64. Gems are one third as plentiful as MS-64s. Some coins are excessively bag marked and should be avoided.

Prooflike examples can be found with little difficulty. Deep mirror prooflike coins are scarce. It's important to consider the presence of die striations on these coins since they do subtract from overall eye appeal. These die lines are common for this issue, but are more distracting on some examples than others.

Echoes of the Past: The last year the mint at Carson City struck a coin was in 1893. Although technically a mint for several years following this stoppage, Carson City was used solely as an assay office, a role it would continue to fill until it was shuttered for good in 1933. That the Carson City Mint occupies a unique position in the history of the Morgan dollar series is undeniable. Its close proximity to the Comstock Lode and its connection to the Old West make its surviving coins national treasures.

In 1900, several unused Carson City dies were returned to Philadelphia and then sent to New Orleans. These were initially struck with Carson City's CC mintmark before being overstruck with the correct O mintmark. The feature is easily visible under a loupe and marks the last time that the famed CC would appear on a U.S. coin.

1900-O
Certified Populations and Check List
Mint State

Circ	MS-60	MS-61	MS-62	MS-63	MS-64	MS-65	MS-66	MS-67	MS-68
462	52	217	2,016	11,050	16,530	5,900	898	40	

Prooflike

Circ	MS-60	MS-61	MS-62	MS-63	MS-64	MS-65	MS-66	MS-67	MS-68
		5	34	110	164	84	24		

Deep Mirror Prooflike

Circ	MS-60	MS-61	MS-62	MS-63	MS-64	MS-65	MS-66	MS-67	MS-68
			2	3	14	13	1		

1900-S

Mintage 3,540,000
Certified Population. 5,352
Prooflike % 4.02
Deep Mirror Prooflike %. 0.17

San Francisco produced more than 3.5 million Morgan dollars in 1900. Like the 1900 Philly strike, some 1900-S dollars were struck with the new C4 reverse hub. The majority of the issue, however, retained the better-defined C3 reverse that had been in use since 1879.

Unfortunately, the 1900-S is considered by some to be the poorest-quality Morgan dollar struck by the San Francisco Mint. Many surviving pieces exhibit a flat, lifeless appearance with weak hair detail on the obverse and washed-out tail feathers on the reverse (an issue exacerbated by the less-defined C4 hub). Planchet striations are also found on some examples.

Many of the issue's better-looking coins came out of the Redfield hoard. Fears that the hoard would dilute the market for the 1900-S proved to be overblown, as it contained only a few bags. Today, the 1900-S is one of the series' better issues.

The typical Uncirculated 1900-S grades from MS-62 to MS-64. PCGS has certified more than 500 pieces in MS-65 and just over 100 examples in grades better. One of the two MS-67s used to reside in Jack Lee's famous set.

Prooflike examples were rare before the Redfield hoard yielded several lightly marked examples. The majority of certified PLs grade below MS-64. Coins with deeper mirrors remain rare.

1900-S
Certified Populations and Check List
Mint State

Circ	MS-60	MS-61	MS-62	MS-63	MS-64	MS-65	MS-66	MS-67	MS-68
734	34	109	571	1,494	1,585	500	99	2	

Prooflike

Circ	MS-60	MS-61	MS-62	MS-63	MS-64	MS-65	MS-66	MS-67	MS-68
	5	6	37	58	83	20	5	1	

Deep Mirror Prooflike

Circ	MS-60	MS-61	MS-62	MS-63	MS-64	MS-65	MS-66	MS-67	MS-68
			1	4	3	1			

1901

Mintage 6,962,000

Certified Population. 4,228

Prooflike % 0.02

Deep Mirror Prooflike %. 0.02

A Great Numismatic Rarity: There's no denying that the time to buy a cheap Mint State example of the coveted Philly strike 1901 dollar has long past. As soon as collectors and dealers realized that almost all of the issue's nearly seven million mintage was lost forever, demand and prices hit record highs.

At the peak of the pre–third-party-grading service coin market, finding a truly Uncirculated 1901 Morgan was tricky business. While true Uncirculated examples of the issue were quite rare, a fair number of lightly circulated sliders were offered to unsuspecting collectors and investors. Widespread acceptance of certified coinage helped clean up this practice, and today we see an accurate illustration of the ratio of About Uncirculated to brilliant Uncirculated examples from this release.

In terms of strike quality, the new C4 reverse did this issue no favors. The coins tend to look flat, and many lack definition in Liberty's hair or on the eagle's breast. In the higher Mint State grades, this characteristic is unforgivable. Of the thousand or so 1901s that survive in Mint State, the average piece grades between MS-61 and MS-63. The most common certified circulated grade is AU-55.

A major doubled-die reverse exists for this issue. It is spectacularly rare in Mint State but routinely offered at auction in grades of Extremely Fine and About Uncirculated.

Impossibly rare to find in quantity in Mint State, the 1901 to date has yielded but a few coins in prooflike and deep mirror prooflike. PCGS has certified one of each, both in the lower MS grade range.

In their long-out-of-print book *What Every Silver Dollar Buyer Should Know* (1984), Steve Ivy and Ron Howard detail 10 frenetic years in the life of the sole MS-63PL, which was first procured from a Mint bag in Montana in the late 1960s and by 1980 had been handled by a proverbial "who's who" of the rare-coin industry, including the likes of Bruce Amspacher, Mike DeFalco, David Hall, Wayne Miller, and Dean Tavenner. The piece went from a $100 bag pull to a coin worth just under $10,000![31]

1901
Certified Populations and Check List

Mint State

Circ	MS-60	MS-61	MS-62	MS-63	MS-64	MS-65	MS-66	MS-67	MS-68
3,632	52	162	234	115	28	3			

Prooflike

Circ	MS-60	MS-61	MS-62	MS-63	MS-64	MS-65	MS-66	MS-67	MS-68
				1					

Deep Mirror Prooflike

Circ	MS-60	MS-61	MS-62	MS-63	MS-64	MS-65	MS-66	MS-67	MS-68
		1							

1901-O

Mintage	13,320,000
Certified Population	26,856
Prooflike %	2.55
Deep Mirror Prooflike %	0.18

The New Orleans Mint was the production leader in 1901, coining 13.3 million Morgan dollars. A fair number circulated at the time, as evidenced by the fact that the coin remains common in all circulated grades. While the bulk of the issue was melted under the Pittman Act, it's estimated that 500,000 or more examples survived in Mint State through the 1960s. Subsequent silver melts have undoubtedly reduced this number.

Quality throughout the issue varies, since many coins were struck with well-worn dies. Multiple reverse hubs were used throughout the year, including at least one instance where dies were made with C4 over C3 hubs! More common is the undoubled C4, with its flat and ill-defined eagle.

When the so-called "Creole" dollars were released in late 1962, the 1901-O was among them. It didn't get the publicity the 1898-O, 1903-O, or 1904-O received because it wasn't considered a major rarity at the time. Today the issue remains plentiful in Mint State through MS-64. Gems are noticeably tougher but still abundant, with just under 3,000 graded by PCGS.

The Treasury release provided collectors the opportunity to cherrypick coveted prooflike and deep mirror prooflike pieces. The 1901-O is readily available in PL, with nearly 700 PCGS-certified examples. In DMPL, the coin is much more scarce; PCGS has certified almost 50.

1901-O
Certified Populations and Check List
Mint State

Circ	MS-60	MS-61	MS-62	MS-63	MS-64	MS-65	MS-66	MS-67	MS-68
223	21	155	1,669	9,386	11,539	2,671	456	3	

Prooflike

Circ	MS-60	MS-61	MS-62	MS-63	MS-64	MS-65	MS-66	MS-67	MS-68
	2	10	47	180	284	150	11		

Deep Mirror Prooflike

Circ	MS-60	MS-61	MS-62	MS-63	MS-64	MS-65	MS-66	MS-67	MS-68
		1	2	18	17	11			

1901-S

Mintage 2,284,000

Certified Population......... 3,426

Prooflike % 0.73

Deep Mirror Prooflike %..... 0.12

The San Francisco Mint struck nearly 2.3 million Morgan dollars in 1901, and thankfully, coin quality was much improved after the poor showing of 1900. Again both C3 and C4 reverse hubs were used, and the C3 almost always exhibits better definition on the eagle's chest and feathers.

Some Mint State examples reveal parallel striations on the highest points of relief. This is believed to have originated during the planchet-making process. (These unsightly marks are even more noticeable on the 1902-S.)

On the market, the 1901-S doesn't get the attention it deserves. Never a great rarity, since there was always some source for them throughout the first half of the 20th century, the issue eluded LaVere Redfield and has not been seen in any original-bag quantity since two turned up in Montana in the early 1960s.[32]

It's been slim pickings since for the issue in Mint State. Circulated pieces up to About Uncirculated are far more likely the norm. In terms of availability, a good analogue is the 1879-CC.

The 1901-S is elusive in prooflike and deep mirror prooflike, but not as spectacularly rare as the 1901 Philly strike. To date, PCGS population reports reveal a total of 25 prooflike pieces, while only a handful have met the strict criteria of the DMPL designation.

1901-S
Certified Populations and Check List
Mint State

Circ	MS-60	MS-61	MS-62	MS-63	MS-64	MS-65	MS-66	MS-67	MS-68
715	20	98	444	993	871	226	29	1	

Prooflike

Circ	MS-60	MS-61	MS-62	MS-63	MS-64	MS-65	MS-66	MS-67	MS-68
		2	6	7	8	2			

Deep Mirror Prooflike

Circ	MS-60	MS-61	MS-62	MS-63	MS-64	MS-65	MS-66	MS-67	MS-68
			1	2	1				

1902

Mintage 7,994,000

Certified Population. 7,134

Prooflike % 0.86

Deep Mirror Prooflike %. 0.01

1902 marked the first full year of coin production at the Philadephia Mint's new facility. The former facility (today as the second mint) had been in use since 1833. Production shifted to the third mint late in 1901. The third Philadelphia Mint took up a city block, had double the capacity of the previous facility, and was well appointed, with seven glass mosaics designed by Louis Tiffany (whose company would later design the 1999 Dolley Madison commemorative dollar). The third mint operated until the early 1970s.

Most of the Morgan dollars struck at the new mint facility in 1902 are long gone; many pieces were immediately entered into circulation but most were melted in 1918. What is available on the market is mostly the result of Treasury releases in the 1950s.

Judging by PCGS population reports, the 1902 is one of Philadelphia's better efforts.

However, those relying primarily on certified grades might miss the fact that the coins themselves do not resemble the better-struck Morgan dollars of years past. This is because the issue marks the first fully exclusive use of the C4 reverse, which lacks definition on the reverse. Luster will appear subdued on a majority of examples, although you can on occasion find a coin or two with lots of flash.

Getting back to grade: the typical 1902 in Mint State will be from MS-62 to MS-65. Lower-grade Mint State pieces may appear heavily bag marked and pancake flat; these are to be avoided as they have no collector upside. Premium-quality, bag-mark-free pieces in the upper range will still appear to be somewhat softly struck.

Semi-prooflike examples are scarce, but truly prooflike coins from this release are rare. To date, PCGS has certified only 61 examples. In deep mirror prooflike the issue is virtually unknown, with only a single example, an MS-63DMPL, residing in a PCGS holder.

1902
Certified Populations and Check List
Mint State

Circ	MS-60	MS-61	MS-62	MS-63	MS-64	MS-65	MS-66	MS-67	MS-68
327	14	49	473	1,651	2,623	1,460	451	24	

Prooflike

Circ	MS-60	MS-61	MS-62	MS-63	MS-64	MS-65	MS-66	MS-67	MS-68
			3	7	27	15	9		

Deep Mirror Prooflike

Circ	MS-60	MS-61	MS-62	MS-63	MS-64	MS-65	MS-66	MS-67	MS-68
				1					

1902-O

Mintage 8,636,000

Certified Population......... 47,729

Prooflike % 1.29

Deep Mirror Prooflike %..... 0.12

In 1902 New Orleans was producing coins at full speed, turning out dimes, quarters, half dollars, and more than 8.6 million Morgan dollars. The additional production capacity of the new facilities in Philadelphia, and new capacity expected from the recently authorized Denver Mint (which would open in 1906 despite numerous delays), were existential threats to the future of Superintendent Hugh Suthon's New Orleans Mint, which had faithfully carried out its duties producing the statute-mandated number of Morgan dollars each and every year since 1879.

In his 1902 *Annual Report*, U.S. Mint Director George Roberts agitated for the closing of the facility, citing redundancy and the fact that the nation's silver stock would soon be used up, ending the need to continue to produce the large dollar coin.[33]

One of a handful of "Creole" dollar dates, the 1902-O was not a great rarity before October 1962, when the Treasury unsealed a vault filled with Morgan dollars struck in New Orleans. After the vault's opening, an abundance of the issue entered the market. It became, and still remains, a common-date Morgan dollar.

In terms of strike quality and luster, the 1902-O rates near the bottom of the entire series. Most examples are flatly struck, greasy in appearance, and bag marked. A miraculous few fully-struck pieces with minimal contact marks survive. Also, several exotic toners, caused by long-term storage in bags over many smoldering Louisiana summers, exist and are definitely worth a look.

The 1902-O is one of the more common late-date Morgans with prooflike surfaces, well represented throughout the midrange of the Mint State scale in PL with more than 100 examples grading gem or better. In deep mirror prooflike the coin is understandably scarcer, but compared to the 1902 Philly or San Francisco strike the 1902-O isn't hard to find certified DMPL.

1902-O
Certified Populations and Check List

Mint State

Circ	MS-60	MS-61	MS-62	MS-63	MS-64	MS-65	MS-66	MS-67	MS-68
137	41	329	3,506	18,231	20,117	4,186	500	9	

Prooflike

Circ	MS-60	MS-61	MS-62	MS-63	MS-64	MS-65	MS-66	MS-67	MS-68
	3	15	73	204	218	90	12		

Deep Mirror Prooflike

Circ	MS-60	MS-61	MS-62	MS-63	MS-64	MS-65	MS-66	MS-67	MS-68
		1	10	18	25	4			

1902-S

Mintage	1,530,000
Certified Population	4,834
Prooflike %	0.74
Deep Mirror Prooflike %	0.02

The San Francisco Mint's primary responsibility in the early years of the 20th century was to process and coin gold bullion extracted from the West Coast and the Yukon. Ancillary to this was the production of silver dollars, of which San Francisco struck 1.5 million pieces in 1902.

As mentioned under the entry for the 1901-S, rolling marks on Liberty's face and sometimes the eagle's breast mar a great number of Mint State 1902-S Morgan dollars. The marks resemble tiny diagonal scratches and cover most of Liberty's face, ear, hair, and Phrygian cap. The diagonal scratches run in the opposite direction.

At least one 1,000-coin bag of 1902-S Morgan dollars was found in the Redfield hoard. The bag was likely cherrypicked before hitting the market, which explains why numismatists in the 1970s and 1980s had differing opinions about the quality and quantity of the issue discovered in that hoard.

PCGS has graded fewer than 5,000 1902-S Morgan dollars, including 900-plus circulated pieces. Most Mint State examples grade MS-63 or MS-64. Gems are scarce due to the faulty planchets, and anything above MS-66 is rare.

The 1902-S is scarce in prooflike and only one has been certified deep mirror prooflike by PCGS. That piece graded MS-62. Of the prooflikes, most straddle either side of MS-63. Two PLs are certified MS-65.

1902-S
Certified Populations and Check List
Mint State

Circ	MS-60	MS-61	MS-62	MS-63	MS-64	MS-65	MS-66	MS-67	MS-68
917	32	100	617	1,415	1,389	290	33	4	

Prooflike

Circ	MS-60	MS-61	MS-62	MS-63	MS-64	MS-65	MS-66	MS-67	MS-68
		5	8	13	8	2			

Deep Mirror Prooflike

Circ	MS-60	MS-61	MS-62	MS-63	MS-64	MS-65	MS-66	MS-67	MS-68
			1						

1903

Mintage 4,652,000

Certified Population 12,981

Prooflike % 0.96

Deep Mirror Prooflike % 0.03

The amount of Sherman Silver Purchase Act bullion on hand was dwindling. At the close of the 1902–1903 fiscal year, the Mint had but 17 million fine ounces on hand and forecast that it would be completely used up in 1904. That forecast proved correct. As an organization the U.S. Mint was readying for the opening of the Denver Mint, which would strike its first coin in 1906. The status of the New Orleans Mint remained in doubt, as the director again repeated his recommendation that the facility be closed and converted to an assay office.[34]

In what would be the antepenultimate year of Morgan dollar production at the Mother Mint, superintendent John Landis and his coiners did a great job, as the 1903 Philly strike is one of the better Philadelphia issues in the series—its only rivals being the 1883 and 1886!

PCGS has graded approximately 13,000 coins from this issue to date, 900 of them being certified at MS-66 and above. Gems are plentiful and the typical certified 1903 grades MS-64.

Most of the Mint State coins were released in the 1950s and 1960s. According to Bowers's research, the coin was scarce before then.[35] Accounts vary as to whether the issue was found in the Redfield hoard. John Love and Wayne Miller recall seeing a small quantity of them, several being prooflike, when the hoard was split up in the 1970s.

However many prooflike coins turned up at that time, they did little to sate collectors' appetites for the mirrored subset of the issue. To date PCGS has graded few more than 100 pieces, with only four meeting the requirements to be attributed deep mirror prooflike. The two best grade MS-65.

1903
Certified Populations and Check List
Mint State

Circ	MS-60	MS-61	MS-62	MS-63	MS-64	MS-65	MS-66	MS-67	MS-68
736	28	112	759	2,839	4,692	2,777	837	73	

Prooflike

Circ	MS-60	MS-61	MS-62	MS-63	MS-64	MS-65	MS-66	MS-67	MS-68
		4	8	31	46	29	6		

Deep Mirror Prooflike

Circ	MS-60	MS-61	MS-62	MS-63	MS-64	MS-65	MS-66	MS-67	MS-68
				1	1	2			

1903-O

Mintage	4,450,000
Certified Population.	11,196
Prooflike %	1.11
Deep Mirror Prooflike %.	0.63

If you were the proud owner of a Mint State 1903-O Morgan dollar in 1960, then you should have been on top of the world. At that point it had only one series rival, the highly coveted 1895 Philadelphia Proof. One could have argued that the 1903-O was much more scarce than its collectors-only cousin. Ah, but it was not to be!

Unbeknownst to everybody, several thousand (no one knows *exactly* how many) were sitting in Mint-sewn bags waiting to be unleashed on the market when the Philadelphia Mint opened its vault of New Orleans dollars. The $1,500 coin ($11,597, adjusted for inflation[36]) was selling for a buck or two over face value within weeks. One shudders to think of the pandemonium that ensued in the days after this issue's release in 1962 and how many unsuspecting shop owners ended up topsy-turvy after buying an example of this erstwhile great rarity.

While no longer one of the key coins of the series, the 1903-O remains an interesting and important part of the Morgan dollar story.

In terms of strike quality, the once-elusive 1903-O is a nice coin if you can find one that isn't flatly struck (many are). Coins released in the 1960s are less bag marked than one would expect, and many have brilliant luster and good eye appeal.

The typical certified grade for the 1903-O is between MS-63 and MS-65. MS-66 examples are plentiful, and 63 have graded MS-67. The issue yielded several prooflike and deep mirror prooflike coins. Many are beautifully struck. Four PLs and four DMPLs have graded MS-66.

1903-O
Certified Populations and Check List
Mint State

Circ	MS-60	MS-61	MS-62	MS-63	MS-64	MS-65	MS-66	MS-67	MS-68
209	34	163	916	2,891	4,065	2,069	592	63	

Prooflike

Circ	MS-60	MS-61	MS-62	MS-63	MS-64	MS-65	MS-66	MS-67	MS-68
	1	3	13	38	47	18	4		

Deep Mirror Prooflike

Circ	MS-60	MS-61	MS-62	MS-63	MS-64	MS-65	MS-66	MS-67	MS-68
			7	17	32	10	4		

1903-S

Mintage 1,241,000

Certified Population......... 2,853

Prooflike % 0.14

Deep Mirror Prooflike %..... 0.00

In the debut edition of the *Red Book*, the 1903-S was the third-most-expensive circulation-strike issue in the series. It even cost $10 more than the 1895 Proof (which allegedly was worth $6 in brilliant Uncirculated, even though circulation strikes for this issue were never made).

As the Morgan dollar market developed, the realization that other dates were more scarce shifted the landscape, and by 1960 the 1903-S was tied with the 1894-P and the 1895-O for 10th place. Today the 1903-S is little moved from that spot—a semi-key date, and perhaps underrated, but not the monster coin it once was.

The issue's 1.24 million–coin mintage was the lowest Morgan dollar output from the San Francisco Mint since it produced a mere 100,000 pieces in 1893. Most of the issue was either melted or circulated, as fewer than 1,500 Mint State examples are believed to survive. Of that total, PCGS has graded just shy of 800 Uncirculated coins.

According to the PCGS population chart, distribution of Uncirculated pieces is most concentrated in the MS-63 to MS-65 range. Excellent luster and minimal bag marks are the norm, especially in the gem grades. One of three MS-67s, a soft-gold-and-orange toner, has been passed down over the years to a who's who of America's greatest collectors, from Clapp to Eliasberg, to Lee, Arno, and Simpson. What a treasure!

Four coins represent the totality of prooflike pieces certified by PCGS. None so far have met the requirement to earn the DMPL designation.

1903-S
Certified Populations and Check List
Mint State

Circ	MS-60	MS-61	MS-62	MS-63	MS-64	MS-65	MS-66	MS-67	MS-68
2,217	2	12	58	155	244	124	34	3	.

Prooflike

Circ	MS-60	MS-61	MS-62	MS-63	MS-64	MS-65	MS-66	MS-67	MS-68
				1	3				

Deep Mirror Prooflike

Circ	MS-60	MS-61	MS-62	MS-63	MS-64	MS-65	MS-66	MS-67	MS-68

1904

Mintage	2,788,000
Certified Population	4,938
Prooflike %	0.61
Deep Mirror Prooflike %	0.04

The majority of Philadelphia's 1904 production was turned out in January as the Mint exhausted the stockpile of silver bullion it bought under the terms of the Sherman Silver Purchase Act. The Mint would strike 66,000 more in February (about a day's worth), and a final 522,000 in June. Were it not for the unexpected resumption of coinage in 1921, the story of the Morgan dollar at the Philadelphia Mint would have ended there.

The bulk of the mintage was sent to the smelter's pot in 1918. It's possible that a few hundred bags circulated, since the coin isn't scarce in well-worn grades. As for Mint State examples, a sufficient number surfaced over the years to convince numismatists that the issue was a semi-common date. Unfortunately, they overestimated the availability of the 1904. While not a rare coin, it is, at the very least, scarce in Mint State. Sliders abound, so be careful when choosing one for your collection.

Another thing to keep in mind is that this release doesn't come nice. Few coins really pack a punch. Weak strike and dull, lifeless luster are the norm, unfortunately. Finding a well–struck, somewhat lustrous coin should be the goal of every serious collector, regardless of grade or price point.

The 1904 is rare in prooflike. When Q. David Bowers published his silver-dollar book in 1993, he stated the known population to be 16 prooflikes and two deep mirror prooflikes at the two major certification services. His belief was that this number accounted for only a tiny *fraction* of the extant population. Twenty years later, PCGS has certified just 30 examples as prooflike and still only the two deep mirror prooflike examples.

The condition-census DMPL was formerly part of Jack Lee's historic Morgan dollar set. It's an MS-65 with high contrast, deep mirrors, and rainbow toning that encircles the outer perimeter.

1904
Certified Populations and Check List
Mint State

Circ	MS-60	MS-61	MS-62	MS-63	MS-64	MS-65	MS-66	MS-67	MS-68
598	50	157	926	1,681	1,256	221	17		

Prooflike

Circ	MS-60	MS-61	MS-62	MS-63	MS-64	MS-65	MS-66	MS-67	MS-68
		1	2	3	7	16	1		

Deep Mirror Prooflike

Circ	MS-60	MS-61	MS-62	MS-63	MS-64	MS-65	MS-66	MS-67	MS-68
					1	1			

1904-O

Mintage 3,720,000

Certified Population 108,784

Prooflike % 2.46

Deep Mirror Prooflike % 0.55

Reversal of Fortune (Part 2): There's simply no denying that the 1904-O, like the 1898-O and the 1903-O, will never return to the vaunted place it held in collectors' hearts before a million or so Uncirculated pieces were released at face value by the Treasury department in 1962. The pre-release Mint State asking price had reached as high as $350, or about $2,660 in today's money.[37][38] For that sum, you can have practically any 1904-O dollar you want, up to MS-66DMPL. It's not very likely that you'd be able to swing an MS-67, as these sell for more, but in 1962 you were lucky to get any example for that price (and I doubt any of the pieces available at the time are even counted in today's top population census, for surely more than a few were likely sliders).

What happened to the 1904-O (and other dates once thought to be scarce) illustrates why it took until the late 1960s and 1970s for the series to really take off. Dealers and collectors were well aware of the immense stockpiles of dollar coins held in government vaults. Until a proper accounting of the government's holdings was undertaken, all the numismatic community could do was guess as to what was left unaccounted for. Mintage totals were irrelevant after the Pittman Act, and the irregular way the coin circulated offered little help gauging how many Mint State examples might exist.

Nevertheless, even though the once-rare New Orleans issues do point out how numisma-

tists got it wrong in terms of scarcity, there are many examples where the opposite is true (see the chapter on the Morgan dollar market). Also, while the picture we currently have of the Morgan dollar series relies on the maturity of third-party certification (there may still be some surprising coins out there), the first outlines of this picture could only take shape after the Treasury releases of the 1960s and the GSA sales in the early 1970s.

The New Orleans Mint: This is where the story of the New Orleans Mint and the Morgan dollar comes to a close. Without the need to produce the big dollar coin, the Mint director eliminated more than half of the facility's staff. The last of the Southern mints continued to strike subsidiary silver coinage and gold coins through 1909, when the Treasury Department forced New Orleans to cease coining operations. The New Orleans Mint was converted to an assay office, which operated up to 1933.

For its final Morgan dollar, New Orleans did well, producing one of the best strikes among O-mint issues from the series. The 1904-O is also one of the most consistently nice coins of the year. The typical Uncirculated piece falls in the MS-62 to MS-64 range. MS-65 gems are available in abundance, but MS-66s are scarce. The issue is rare at MS-67.

1904 is the most common New Orleans prooflike issue (although the 1881 and 1883 to1885 are better dates for DMPLs). The majority of PLs grade MS-63 or MS-64. Hairlines and bag marks preclude most from being gems. This also applies to deep mirror prooflikes. One truly exceptional piece, an MS-67DMPL, currently resides in the superlative Levi Ranch collection.

1904-O
Certified Populations and Check List
Mint State

Circ	MS-60	MS-61	MS-62	MS-63	MS-64	MS-65	MS-66	MS-67	MS-68
128	70	711	6,943	39,140	47,061	10,610	818	31	

Prooflike

Circ	MS-60	MS-61	MS-62	MS-63	MS-64	MS-65	MS-66	MS-67	MS-68
	6	27	195	821	1,123	436	63		

Deep Mirror Prooflike

Circ	MS-60	MS-61	MS-62	MS-63	MS-64	MS-65	MS-66	MS-67	MS-68
		7	46	174	247	107	19	1	

1904-S

Mintage 2,304,000

Certified Population 2,977

Prooflike % 0.94

Deep Mirror Prooflike % 0.00

The 2.3 million Morgan dollars produced by the San Francisco Mint in 1904 sputtered out in two separate two-month bursts. A little more than 1.46 million were struck in January and February, and 836,000 more were produced in April and May. Ultimately, a large percentage of the issue was likely melted, since only a few Mint-sewn bags have ever been reported, and those were last seen in the first half of the 20th century. The cache of Uncirculated dollars provided by these releases was enough to supply the relatively small Morgan dollar collector base until the numbers of collectors exploded in the 1950s and 1960s. By 1963 the issue had climbed in value to $50.

The 1904-S isn't one of San Francisco's finest issues. The typical example may have good luster and frosty surfaces, but strike tends to be mediocre—resembling a Philadelphia product rather than one from the esteemed San Francisco Mint. Bag marks also heavily impact the eye appeal of the issue, as most coins have a number of surface abrasions that keep them from obtaining grades higher than choice. PCGS has graded only 11 higher than MS-66.

The erstwhile "final" San Francisco Morgan dollar is rare in prooflike and deep mirror prooflike. Only 28 coins have earned a PL designation from PCGS, and no DMPLs have been certified to date.

1904-S
Certified Populations and Check List
Mint State

Circ	MS-60	MS-61	MS-62	MS-63	MS-64	MS-65	MS-66	MS-67	MS-68
1,718	13	61	212	397	413	124	9	2	

Prooflike

Circ	MS-60	MS-61	MS-62	MS-63	MS-64	MS-65	MS-66	MS-67	MS-68
		1	4	9	10	3	1		

Deep Mirror Prooflike

Circ	MS-60	MS-61	MS-62	MS-63	MS-64	MS-65	MS-66	MS-67	MS-68

1921

Mintage 44,690,000

Certified Population. 70,217

Prooflike % 0.42

Deep Mirror Prooflike % 0.02

After a hiatus of 17 years, the Morgan dollar returned to production in 1921 due to provisions in the Pittman Act, which had authorized the government to melt silver dollars and sell the recovered bullion to Great Britain. The condition was that the U.S. government would repurchase that same amount of bullion and recoin silver dollars. Britain used the silver to prop up the Indian rupee (India was then a British colony) during World War I.

In total, 270,232,722 silver dollars (259,121,554 of them earmarked for Britain) were melted, with the government first melting "free stock" dollars, which were coins that were not struck to back outstanding Silver Certificates. Meanwhile, the Federal Reserve banks

went into action to replace Silver Certificates with Federal Reserve Bank Notes to free the remaining inventory.

The decision to re-coin the Morgan dollar was not without its opponents. Bills were introduced to repeal the repurchase clause, but all of them failed. In May of 1920 the price of silver bullion dipped below $1.00 per ounce, triggering the purchase of new bullion.

A Necessary Design Change: In 1910, six years after the cessation of its coinage, the U.S. Mint saw no further need to maintain or store Morgan dollar hubs, so most were destroyed. This proved problematic in 1921, when the Mint had to strike new Morgan dollars. So new lower-relief hubs were created, using the 1878 7TF PAF as the model.[39] The resulting coin was a pale imitation of the original dollar design. Morgan's eventual successor, John Sinnock, is said to have assisted with the preparation of the hubs.

For Morgan dollar enthusiasts, the 1921 will probably never be a favorite due to the above-mentioned design differences and because of its colossal mintage. The 1921 output from all three mints represents nearly 44 percent of the total mintage of the series, taking out the coins lost to the Pittman Act melt.

That said, the coin is still numismatically interesting and important in its own right. The 17-year production hiatus would happen again in U.S. history, with the 1999 mintage of the Susan B. Anthony dollar. That coin, like the Morgan, was holed up in government vaults for years. Dwindling supplies of the Suzie B. forced its improbable re-coining a year before the introduction of the Sacagawea golden dollar. Like the 1921 Morgan, the 1999 Anthony dollar was struck using dies from new hubs.

Another interesting aspect of the 1921 dollar was that it was transitioned out at the end of the year by Anthony de Francisci's Peace dollar design, which was the result of lobbying by several prominent members of the American Numismatic Association (who, ironically, weren't pleased with the final design).

The end of the Morgan dollar series brought to a close a fascinating era of American coinage. The new "Peace" design embodied the new Saint-Gaudens–inspired period, which some consider the epoch of American numismatic design.

The Coin: Released in quantity through 1964, the quality of the 1921 varies based on strike and the number of marks on the coin's surface. Although purists may disagree, attractive examples do exist. Uncirculated examples likely fall in the MS-62 to MS-64 range. Gems are plentiful but the coin becomes scarce in MS-66 and above. Mike Casper, a serious Morgan dollar enthusiast, considers the sole MS-67PL to be the best 1921 Morgan dollar from any of the mints. He and Jack Lee both had the privilege of owning this museum-quality piece at one time.

Speaking of prooflike and deep mirror prooflike Morgans, the issue yields few examples with mirrors or cameos. In DMPL the coin is extremely scarce, with 14 pieces attributed by PCGS and only one gem. Abrasions usually limit the eye appeal of the known DMPLs. The coin fares better in PL, with 14 examples in gem or above (including the Lee/Casper piece).

1921
Certified Populations and Check List
Mint State

Circ	MS-60	MS-61	MS-62	MS-63	MS-64	MS-65	MS-66	MS-67	MS-68
2,014	58	456	8,572	29,691	24,756	4,010	346	7	

Prooflike

Circ	MS-60	MS-61	MS-62	MS-63	MS-64	MS-65	MS-66	MS-67	MS-68
	2	12	57	116	92	12	1	1	

Deep Mirror Prooflike

Circ	MS-60	MS-61	MS-62	MS-63	MS-64	MS-65	MS-66	MS-67	MS-68
		3	1	3	6	1			

1921-D

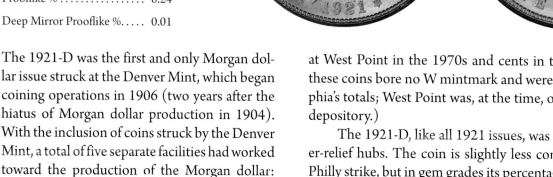

Mintage 20,345,000

Certified Population......... 14,291

Prooflike % 0.24

Deep Mirror Prooflike %..... 0.01

The 1921-D was the first and only Morgan dollar issue struck at the Denver Mint, which began coining operations in 1906 (two years after the hiatus of Morgan dollar production in 1904). With the inclusion of coins struck by the Denver Mint, a total of five separate facilities had worked toward the production of the Morgan dollar: Philadelphia, Carson City, New Orleans, San Francisco, and now Denver.

The Morgan dollar would be the last circulating coin struck by more than three different mints until the West Point Mint (in New York) struck a collector-release-only 1996-W dime to commemorate the Roosevelt dime's 50th anniversary. (Although quarter dollars were struck

at West Point in the 1970s and cents in the 1970s and 1980s, these coins bore no W mintmark and were included in Philadelphia's totals; West Point was, at the time, officially just a bullion depository.)

The 1921-D, like all 1921 issues, was struck from new lower-relief hubs. The coin is slightly less common than the 1921 Philly strike, but in gem grades its percentages are comparable to the aforementioned Philadelphia release. The typical 1921-D in Uncirculated condition grades from MS-62 to MS-64.

One major difference between the 1921-D and the 1921-P is how much rarer Denver prooflike and deep mirror prooflike coins are (not that PLs and DMPLs are at all common from the Mother Mint). PCGS has graded just one example in DMPL, an MS-64DMPL.

1921-D
Certified Populations and Check List
Mint State

Circ	MS-60	MS-61	MS-62	MS-63	MS-64	MS-65	MS-66	MS-67	MS-68
1,181	44	176	1,561	4,488	5,022	1,521	257	6	

Prooflike

Circ	MS-60	MS-61	MS-62	MS-63	MS-64	MS-65	MS-66	MS-67	MS-68
		1	3	3	10	14	3		

Deep Mirror Prooflike

Circ	MS-60	MS-61	MS-62	MS-63	MS-64	MS-65	MS-66	MS-67	MS-68
					1				

1921-S

Mintage	21,695,000
Certified Population	10,523
Prooflike %	0.07
Deep Mirror Prooflike %	0.00

The Morgan dollar began its swan song when coinage at the San Francisco Mint started on May 9, 1921. By striking Morgan dollars in 1921, the San Francisco Mint holds the unique position of being the only mint facility to make circulation-strike Morgan dollars for each year of its production run.

Like the other 1921 issues, the 1921-S gets a bad rap due to its large mintage. And yes, there are more than enough 1921-S Morgan dollars to go around. However, the quantity of coins bearing a date and mintmark is not always congruent to the number of desirable coins with the same features. In this respect, the 1921-S is underrated.

In gem grades, the issue is scarcer than the 1886-S (750,000 coins struck) and the 1889-S (700,000 coins struck). PCGS has graded only 38 in MS-66 and none finer. MS-65 gems are somewhat more plentiful, but they aren't nearly enough to satisfy thousands of Morgan dollar collectors. The typical Uncirculated coin grades from MS-62 to MS-64—a far cry from the San Francisco Mint's heyday, and all the more reason for collectors to take this final Morgan dollar issue seriously.

It is exceptionally rare in prooflike, and is not known to exist in deep mirror prooflike. PCGS has recognized just seven 1921-S dollars as being PL. Borderline prooflike coins or coins with a prooflike obverse or reverse do exist in greater quantity, but in only a handful of instances has a coin had what it takes to earn the PL designation.

1921-S
Certified Populations and Check List
Mint State

Circ	MS-60	MS-61	MS-62	MS-63	MS-64	MS-65	MS-66	MS-67	MS-68
1,090	19	101	1,320	3,684	3,492	772	38		

Prooflike

Circ	MS-60	MS-61	MS-62	MS-63	MS-64	MS-65	MS-66	MS-67	MS-68
			3	3	1				

Deep Mirror Prooflike

Circ	MS-60	MS-61	MS-62	MS-63	MS-64	MS-65	MS-66	MS-67	MS-68

Chapter Five

Morgan Dollar Proofs

More so than today, in the 19th century coins played a dual role in promoting the national interest. First and foremost, coins were stores of wealth and facilitators of commerce. A nation could not grow or sustain its economic strength without a healthy supply of honest coinage.

But coins also played an important symbolic role. The proper confluence of art and craft projected a nation's power, influence, and prestige, both at home and abroad. This secondary aspect of coinage has been intertwined with the first throughout history. Understanding and interpreting these symbols is one of the main draws of numismatics.

Dr. Henry Linderman, twice director of the United States Mint and a financier by trade, understood well the importance of design and found the nation's coinage lacking in technical and aesthetic merit. He felt that his engravers weren't capable of matching or surpassing the designs of our European counterparts. To rem-

edy this, Linderman sought help from the British Royal Mint's deputy master, William Freemantle, who recommended the U.S. Mint hire the up-and-coming 31-year-old engraver George T. Morgan.

Morgan's arrival in Philadelphia was met by resentment and attempts at sabotage by Chief Engraver William Barber, who perhaps acted out of professional jealousy and fear that the interloper Morgan might supplant his son as the Mint's next chief engraver. Whatever Barber's motives, Morgan's eventual design for the dollar was a result of studying and working off site.

Upon seeing Morgan's sketches, Director Linderman believed that a heightened aesthetic had been achieved. Morgan was ordered to make models, and a number of revisions were made to the design. The Mint had a year-and-a-half head start on the passage of the Bland-Allison Act. By the time Congress overrode President Rutherford Hayes's veto, the coin was ready to enter production.

The first coins struck were Proofs, the first of which was presented to President Hayes in Washington, D.C. That piece, an 1878, Eight Tail Feathers Proof, currently resides at the Hayes Presidential Library in Fremont, Ohio.

Morgan Proof Diagnostics

Proof or not a Proof? Believe it or not, reliable, industry-accepted standards regarding the identifying characteristics of Morgan dollar Proofs are a relatively recent development. Throughout the first half of the 20th century, dealers and collectors commonly misattributed circulation-strike Morgan dollars (presumably prooflikes or deep mirror prooflikes) as *bona fide* Proofs. Still more collectors misunderstood the term "Proof" as a description of a coin's condition, and not as a coin derived from a special production process.

Today, when numismatists describe the identifying features of a Proof Morgan dollar, they use the following four characteristics:

1. **Square Rims.** Circulation strikes have rims that appear rounded under magnification. Proofs, on the other hand, have rims that present a flattened appearance, the result of striking multiple times with extra pressure. Also, in nearly all cases, the dentils will appear fully separated from the rim.

2. **Mirrored Fields.** Proof Morgans have deeply reflective mirrored fields, more so than deep mirror prooflike circulation strikes. This is the result of using polished dies and specially prepared planchets. Furthermore, Proof Morgans should not appear bag marked, as these coins were specially manufactured and sold individually. Improperly handled Proofs can have hairlines, however.

3. **Superior Detail.** With some exceptions, Morgan Proofs are sharply struck coins with full detail on the eagle's chest feathers and (usually) atop the ear.

4. **Coiner's Intent.** This also could be read as the Mint's intent. Simply put, does the coin have the above-mentioned features and was it struck with the purpose of showing its design with maximum clarity? Was the coin struck for the purpose of being circulated in the economy? If so, it's *probably* not a Proof. Was the coin struck for the purpose of being a presentation piece? If so, it's likely a Proof.

A grey area in numismatics exists where Morgan dollars with Proof characteristics have appeared from the branch mints but no documentation relating to their origin is known. Regardless of their "official" status, these pieces are intriguing and highly sought after.

It would take an entire book to describe the complexities of Morgan dollar Proofs. For the collector interested in learning more about this fascinating area of numismatics, I present the following summary information about each year's Proof issue.

1878

It's been said about Proofs that they are the "coiner's caviar;" that is, they are the elevation of the form to its highest level of technical and artistic merit. Because of the special care and refined technique required to strike them, Proofs offer numismatists the opportunity to examine a coin that is as close to the engraver's original vision as is technologically possible.

In 1858, the Mint under J.R. Snowden began to produce Proof coins in quantity for sale to collectors through the Treasury. Before this, Proofs were occasionally given as presentation pieces to dignitaries and the well connected, and were made available to numismatists upon application. While the size of the numismatic community in the 1850s was minuscule compared to the number of active collectors today, enough demand existed for the Mint to strike hundreds of Proof coins, which were typically sold in sets. With rare exception, Proof coining was done at the Philadelphia Mint.

When the Morgan dollar debuted in 1878, the Mint offered three different Proof set options: a nickel-brass minor denomination set, a silver set (with the nickel-brass coins included), and a gold set. The silver set, having been delivered to the Treasury for sale in January (one month before the authorization of the Morgan dollar), did not include the new dollar coin, but instead featured the trade dollar. The Morgan dollar Proof was sold separately. The cost per coin was $1.25 plus postage—unless you picked it up in person, in which case postage need not apply.

According to available records, the first delivery of Morgan Proofs occurred on Tuesday, March 12, when the Treasury accepted delivery of 100 pieces. These coins were likely struck shortly after the aforementioned Hayes piece. 100 additional Proof coins arrived later in the week, followed by another 100 on Monday, March 18.

After this point, numismatists are split. Some, such as the editors of the *Red Book* and the experts at PCGS, state that a total of 500 1878, Eight Tail Feathers, Morgans were struck, probably citing a final March delivery of 200 coins on March 26. Others, extrapolating from Mint records, say that only 300 1878 8TF Proofs were struck, and that the remaining Proof production for the year comprised of two varieties of the amended 7TF reverse.

Given the number of pieces extant in the marketplace after almost 140 years, it's a moot point since the debate has little material effect on the market. The 1878 8TF is the most common of the three, followed by the 1878 7TF, Reverse of 1878, and finally the rare 1878 7TF, Reverse of 1879.

1879

The silver Mint set of 1879 contained seven pieces. Dropped from the set was the trade dollar, which had been replaced by the Morgan dollar, and the 20-cent piece, which had been discontinued. The trade dollar, like the Morgan of a year before, was offered separately at a cost of $1.25. As a standalone product, the trade dollar Proof proved to be more popular than the Proof set, with a mintage of 1,541.

Published Morgan Proof mintage figures suggest that 1,100 coins were struck, but this figure may be high. To date, PCGS has graded just 304 examples. Quality is much improved over the previous year's offering. Most examples are brilliant, but a handful have deeply frosted cameo devices. Dark toning is typical.

1880

The Mint struck 1,440 Morgan Proofs for the 1880 silver Proof set. 1,355 sets were sold, while the remaining 85 coins were melted. The net mintage for the date makes the 1880 the most common Proof in the series. Quality is generally excellent, and cameo examples of this date range from antiqued and yellowed to drop-dead gorgeous and white as 15 feet of freshly fallen snow. Trust your instincts when looking at beautiful coins from this issue, as bid prices do not take wonder coins into account.

1881

Quality took yet another step up in 1881. Proofs in 1881 show stronger detail, especially in the eagle's breast area and the wreath, where the leaves have a fleshy, lifelike appearance. Rims are wider and more squared, and the coin generally boasts attractive, highly mirrored fields.

Production was off from the year before due to lower demand. The total number of coins distributed was 33 percent lower than in 1880. 975 Morgan dollars were sold in sets, while the additional nine pieces were presumably sold as singles. 105 Morgans went unsold and were melted; they do not figure in this issue's mintage.

1882

This issue boasts several exquisite deep cameo examples and many frosty cameos. Quality is again excellent, so long as the coins weren't improperly cleaned or carelessly handled. The Mint struck 1,150 or 1,151 pieces, depending on your source, but a disparity of one coin is nothing to get too excited about. Fifty of these went unsold and were melted. Some Proofs from this date feature doubling on the 82 of the date.

1883

Midway through the Mint's six-year run of truly excellent Proof strikes (1880 to 1885) comes the 1883 Morgan Proof. 1,075 were struck over the course of the year, and 1,039 of those were distributed. Roughly half survive today. PCGS has graded 281 pieces, 63 of which earned a PF-65 or better!

Cameos exist but few deep cameos survive. To date, PCGS has graded two. One is a black-and-white stunner, and the other is a vivid "target" toner in rich blue, orange, and red. Both coins graded PF-66DCAM.

1883 was an interesting year for Proof collectors as the Mint struck three different Proof nickels: the 1883 Shield nickel, the disastrous 1883 Liberty Head Without CENTS design, and the 1883 Liberty Head with CENTS. An original set that sold in 2011 contained the first two designs, but not the third.

1884

The entire run of 1884 Proof Morgans was struck with one set of Proof dies. 920 were produced, but 45 didn't sell and were later melted. Fewer certified examples of this issue exist than one might think. At latest count, PCGS has graded 255.

A select few heavily frosted deep cameo pieces survive. The finest example PCGS has certified, a PF-67DCAM, sold in April 2013 at the Central States Numismatic Society Signature Auction, bringing $28,200. Cameos are more common. PCGS has certified 56 to date, the best also grading PF-67.

Most surviving coins are toned and poor handling has damaged many. Cleaned coins with hairlines are a problem. The average example PCGS has seen grades in the PF-63 to PF-64 range.

1885

933 Morgan dollar Proofs were struck in 1885, with only three going unsold and probably being melted. Issue quality is on par with others dated 1880 to 1885, meaning that most coins are well struck, deeply mirrored, and attractive. PCGS has certified nearly 30 percent of the total mintage, which includes a high percentage of cameos (64 pieces). Deep cameos are rare and only two have been certified; both are PF-65DCAMs.

1886

A total of 891 Morgan Proofs were struck in 1886, with 886 of them distributed in silver Proof sets. The remaining five pieces are believed to have been melted. As is the case with all Morgan Proofs, a considerable number have been lost to time or carelessness. Because of this, the attrition rate is believed to be about 50 to 60 percent.

Some numismatists contend that Morgan dollar Proofs dated 1886 to 1891 lack the punch of Proofs struck earlier in the series. We do see a clear drop in the number of frosted cameos, which go from 30 percent of PCGS-graded examples from 1886 to just over 15 percent of the total graded population from 1887. Some, like the top-pop PF-67CAM, exhibit doubling on the 18 and the 6, along with a thick dash that juts out from beneath the second eight.

1887

Production of Proof sets tapered off by nearly 20 percent in 1887. In total, 710 Morgan Proofs were struck and distributed, the majority of which were brilliant Proofs with adequate mirrors and device details. Several exceptional pieces survive. PCGS has certified 20 pieces as PF-66 or better, with three of those being cameos. Despite a lower mintage, the availability of this issue is on par with those of earlier years. PCGS has graded 39 percent of the total mintage, perhaps indicating a higher than expected survival rate. Many coins are darkly toned, as one would expect given the storage media and techniques of the time.

The finest known is a jade and aubergine-colored stunner graded PF-68.

1888

The 1888 Proof was once considered underrepresented in the marketplace compared to its mintage of 833 coins. This is no longer the case. Make no mistake, however; no more than 50 to 60 percent of the mintage survives in uncompromised condition. As a type coin, the 1888 is not the strongest representation of the series. Many Proofs exhibit weaknesses above Liberty's ear, and the eagle's breast feathers lack the pop of coins made from 1880 to 1885.

PCGS has graded 25 percent of the total mintage, and most exhibit some degree of toning. Cameos make up a little more than one-fifth of the total population. Three examples share the top-pop PF-66CAM grade, of which one sold for $24,675 at the April 2013 Central States Numismatic Society's Signature Auction. A lone deep cameo example sits on PCGS's population report. It's a PF-64DCAM.

1889

The mintage of Morgan dollar Proofs held at right above 800 coins before a two-year drought. Again, the surviving uncompromised population is approximately twice the number of PCGS's current graded total, which sits at 224. The same problems that affect the 1888 also affect the 1889. Weak detail in the highest points of relief are a factor for 1889 Morgan dollar Proofs, which means even the fussiest collector may have to make some compromises.

PCGS has certified 47 examples as cameo, which is par for the course. A lone PF-68CAM sits atop the population report. It's a richly toned coin bathed in port wine, russet, and cobalt-blue toning.

1890

Interest in silver Proof sets hit a nadir in 1890, with just 590 sets sold. This makes the 1890 Morgan dollar Proof the lowest-produced date of the series (though each of the three 1878 Proof varieties is individually scarcer), which historically has been a boon for speculators. Level-headed collectors might look at the PCGS population report and see that the surviving population of the coin is similar to most other Morgan Proofs produced up to this point. To date, PCGS has graded 234 Morgan Proofs from 1890, of which 56 are cameos and 10 are deep cameos.

Two things the issue has going for it are a return to pre-1886 quality standards and a strong selection of pieces graded PF-65 and better (roughly a quarter of PCGS's certified population of 1890 Morgan Proofs falls into this category).

1891

Striking inconsistencies mar this issue. Some coins are adequately struck, while others are soft, especially around Liberty's ear and bangs. The eagle's chest feathers also tend to exhibit weakness. More than half of the 650 minted Proofs from this issue survive in gradable condition. Most examples are darkly toned, and only about a quarter of extant pieces have earned a cameo designation. A single coin, graded at PF-66DCAM, brought $25,300 at the 2005 FUN Signature Auction.

Arguably the finest surviving piece from this issue once belonged in the JFS Collection. It's a toned cameo PF-68CAM, with deep mirrors and hints of original white color underneath a sophisticated medley of grape and wine toning.

1892

Strike softness continued to plague this issue, although a minority of fully struck examples exist. The total mintage for this date (1,245) is more than double the output of the year before, likely driven by the introduction of the new Barber issues. To date, PCGS has graded 32 percent of the total mintage, with the majority grading PF-63 or PF-64. Cameos make up roughly 16 percent of the year's total mintage. Deep cameos are rare.

1893

The Mint began to use hydraulic presses for the striking of Proofs starting in 1893. The presses would later be used to greater effect, but for Morgan dollars from 1893, the results were less than optimal. Some rate as the weakest-struck Proofs in the entire Morgan dollar Proof series.

There are, however, noticeable exceptions. These include one exceptional PF-68CAM and an absolutely miraculous PF-69DCAM, both of which are among the best-struck examples of the issue.

Despite the strike softness, 1893 is one of the better dates so far in the series for cameos and deep cameos. PCGS has certified 260 Morgan dollar Proofs from 1893; of those, 50 are attributed cameo and 9 are designated deep cameo.

1894

While no longer the case, collectors of the late-19th and early-20th centuries considered Proof strikes interchangeable with circulation strikes—especially for tough issues like the 1894, with its paltry mintage of 110,000 coins. This led to many 1894 silver Proof sets being broken up. Nowadays, it's quite rare to find original Proof sets, although several have been re-assembled.

The 1894 Morgan dollar Proof features a much-improved strike when compared to the Morgan Proofs that preceded it in 1892 and 1893. Hair details are well defined, and contrast is much more apparent on coins with light to no toning.

PCGS has graded 339 examples, approximately 35 percent of the total mintage. Most grade PF-63 or PF-64. The few ultra-high-end pieces that exist are showstoppers at auctions.

1895

For nearly 100 years, it was assumed that the reported mintage of 12,000 circulation strikes from 1895 was accurate, and that for whatever reason (usually considered due to the Pittman Act), those circulation strikes never turned up. The great Treasury releases of the 1950s and 1960s failed to uncover any, and it's safe to assume that if any are in collectors' hands then the value of the coins would surely bring them to market (the 1933 Saint-Gaudens double eagle turned up, and that coin was illegal to own!).

What *would* an authentic circulation-strike 1895 sell for today? Five million dollars? Ten million? The mind swoons.

The more recent consensus is that the stated 12,000 struck was some sort of clerical error, or at the very least a mistaken interpretation of Mint reports. It's thought that the coins were, in fact, never struck, and the 880 Proof coins represent the totality of Philadelphia's Morgan dollar output for 1895. It is this legacy that drives the price of this essential Morgan Proof issue.

PCGS has certified 57.5 percent of the total mintage of 1895 dollars, including 103 impaired Proofs graded from an unheard-of PF-6 (no, that's not a typo) on up to PF-58. One hundred examples earned either cameo or deep cameo designations, with the finest known—a black-and-white PF-68DCAM—bringing more than $120,000 in a July 2003 auction.

1896

118 fewer silver Proof sets were produced in 1896 than in 1895, but the fact that a ready supply of Mint State circulation strikes exists releases some of the price pressure on the 1896 that the aforementioned 1895 Proof experiences.

Quality for the issue is much improved, as the series enters a second period of excellence (the first being 1880 to 1886). This run of great coins lasts from 1896 to 1898. PCGS has graded 39 percent of the original mintage, from which 17 percent earned the cameo designation, and a robust 10 percent earned deep cameo. If you want to add a thickly frosted Morgan dollar Proof to your collection, this is one of the best dates to choose from.

This issue is also notable for the high number of well-preserved coins in PF-65 and above.

1897

For those looking for just one example of the Morgan dollar in Proof, the 1897 has it all: quality, affordability, and numerous examples in high grades.

In 1897, the Philadelphia Mint continued where it left off in 1896, turning out excellent Proof coinage. The coins speak for themselves; one in ten Morgan dollar Proofs have enough cameo to earn the designation (DCAMs are rare, however). After grading 37 percent of the total mintage, PCGS has noted that one in five gradable Proofs has graded PF-65 or above! Quite impressive for a 115-year-old coin.

Of minor consequence, the date displays some microscopic doubling.

1898

It's a toss-up as to which issue, 1897 or 1898, is better in terms of mirrors, strike, quality, and preservation. While the 1897 typically comes better preserved (by a point, by PCGS's records), 1898 is the clear winner when it comes to eye appeal, toning, and cameo contrast. Some Proofs are so nice that their surfaces look wet.

The tale of the numbers: PCGS has graded 37 percent of the total mintage. The average grade ranges from PF-63 to PF-64, with several pieces grading higher. 10 percent are cameos, and an astounding 17 percent are deep cameos.

1899

1899, like 1894, is a low-mintage date for Philadelphia circulation strikes. However, the two coins could not be farther apart on the collector market, as the '99 isn't hard to obtain. The 1899 Proof, with a healthy mintage of 846 pieces, is also affordable as Proof Morgan dollars go.

PCGS has graded 288 pieces, or 34 percent of the entire mintage. Most of them grade between PF-62 to PF-64, but several have graded PF-65 or better. This includes a pair of exquisitely toned PF-68s, bathed in colors of absinthe, marmalade, and jade.

One in six 1899 Proofs graded by PCGS has earned the cameo designation; 2 percent have earned deep cameo.

Of note: die-polish marks are sometimes visible on Liberty's face.

1900

The year 1900 saw the production of 912 silver Proof sets, slightly more than the year before but not as significant an increase as one might expect. Perhaps our relatives at the turn of the century weren't as sentimental about the coming of the new century as we are today. Or maybe the sets cost too much. While not as flashy as the 1898 or 1899, the 1900 Proof is adequately struck, but there is a decrease in contrast between the devices and fields.

Properly cared for examples likely make up half of the total mintage. PCGS has certified 30.3 percent, which is on par for most dates in the series. From that total, 16 percent are cameos and only 8 coins (3 percent) earned deep cameo.

The typical gradable example falls in the PF-62 to PF-64 range. Strikes are above average, and astute observers might notice the Very Near Date Set Low obverse (VAM-7).

1901

The scarcity of high-grade, Uncirculated 1901 Philadelphia circulation strikes has traditionally put pressure on the price of the '01 Proof. Matters only got worse when the 1901 didn't turn up in any significant quantity during the Treasury releases of the 1950s and 1960s. Today, the issue still feels pricing pressure, but to a lesser extent because of changes in collector behavior (Proof issues and circulation strikes no longer being collected interchangeably).

The degree of cameo contrast continued to decline, and even the better examples can show weakness on the eagle's wing feathers. Van Allen and Mallis cite the new C4 reverses and changes to the fuel used in the Mint's annealing furnace. Whatever the cause, from this point onward until the end of the series, finding deep contrast between the devices and fields is difficult.

PCGS has graded 294 Proofs in all grades (36 percent of the mintage). From that population, 12 percent are cameo, and none have earned the vaunted deep cameo.

1902

Unfortunately, the final few Proof issues of the Morgan dollar series lack the splash and technical expertise of many of the earlier ones. This is especially true of the 1902, which exhibits virtually no hint of contrast and tends to display a copper-tinged, highly polished appearance. Numismatist Mike Fuljenz correctly attributes this look as being "chromed."

777 pieces were struck, and most gradable pieces fall in the PF-62 to PF-64 range. Cameos are rare. PCGS has certified only three, with none in deep cameo; with 260 Proofs graded, the odds of finding more are low.

1903

In the penultimate year of production (before a long hiatus), the 1903 Proof compares favorably to the '02 and '04, but is hardly a series standout. Non-compromised pieces continue to have a "chromed" appearance (as described in the entry for 1902) and offer little in the way of contrast.

With 39 percent of the total mintage of 755 coins certified by PCGS, the 1903 Morgan dollar Proof is represented by 20 or more examples in PF-61 to PF-66, the highest concentration falling between PF-62 and PF-64. A select few cameos exist but deep cameos are non-existent.

1904

Technically, this is the last Proof issue. Some might quibble and call the Zerbe/Chapman pieces of 1921 Proofs. I disagree. The 1904 Proof Morgan dollar has always been a coveted coin. Not to the same degree as the 1895, obviously, but desired nonetheless, because it represents the end of the line for George T. Morgan's 26-year-long silver-dollar series.

It is believed that the Mint distributed only 650 silver Proof sets in 1904, which makes this issue the scarcest outside of the three separate Proof styles of 1878.

Quality-wise, the series goes out with a whimper. Minimal contrast, coppery-tinged chrome toning (although there are some gorgeous rainbows to be found, for a price), and so-so strikes are characteristic of the issue. Cameos exist but look as if they were struck by accident. PCGS has graded just one since the company's debut in 1986. That coin is a darkly toned PF-65CAM.

PCGS has certified 56 percent of the total mintage, which comprises most of the non-compromised Proofs for the issue. PF-62 to PF-64 is typical.

Notes

CHAPTER 3

1. Van Allen, Leroy C., and A. George Mallis. *Comprehensive Catalog and Encyclopedia of Morgan and Peace Dollars* (Orlando, Florida: Worldwide Ventures, 1991), 401.
2. Highfill, John. *The Comprehensive U.S. Silver Dollar Encyclopedia* (Broken Arrow, Oklahoma: Highfill Press, 1992), 60.
3. Auction held January 27 and 28, 1986.
4. http://www.coinweek.com/numismatic-history/coin-collecting-or-investing-with-david-hall-and-john-ford-in-1989/.

CHAPTER 4

1. Breen, Walter. *Walter Breen's Complete Encyclopedia of U.S. and Colonial Coins* (New York: Doubleday, 1988); and www.pcgscoinfacts.com.
2. Yeoman, R.S. *A Guide Book of United States Coins,* 67th ed. (Atlanta: Whitman Publishing, 2013).
3. All certified populations in this chapter are from www.pcgs.com, accessed May 31, 2013, except as noted otherwise; population figures for this coin were accessed June 1, 2013.
4. Professional Coin Grading Service (PCGS).
5. Shafer, Neil. "The Morgan Silver Dollars, 1878–1921," *The Whitman Numismatic Journal* (November 1964).
6. *Annual Report of the Director of the Mint,* 1879.
7. http://data.bls.gov/cgi-bin/cpicalc.pl.
8. *Annual Report of the Director of the Mint,* 1881.
9. Van Allen and Mallis, *Comprehensive Catalog and Encyclopedia.*
10. *Annual Report of the Director of the Mint,* 1883.
11. Figure based on a comparison of the Consumer Price Indices of 1883 to 2013. Source: http://data.bls.gov/cgi-bin/cpicalc.pl.
12. Ibid.
13. Yeoman, R.S. *A Guide Book of United States Coins.* (Racine, Wisconsin: Whitman Publishing, 1960).
14. Personal conversation with the author, June 2013.
15. *Coin Dealer Newsletter,* December 22, 1967.
16. www.pcgs.com, accessed July 2013.
17. Bowers, Q. David. *Silver Dollars and Trade Dollars of the United States.* (Wolfeboro, New Hampshire: Bowers and Merena Galleries, 1993).
18. http://data.bls.gov/cgi-bin/cpicalc.pl.
19. Mehl, B. Max. "The Most Extraordinary Collection of U.S. Large Cents…," *The Numismatic Scrapbook Magazine* (August 20, 1959): 685.
20. Diehl, Philip. Personal correspondence, December 2, 2013. "One and only one reason: our demand forecast showed that we might run out of SBAs before the Sacagawea dollar was ready to launch."
21. *Annual Report of the Director of the Mint,* 1889.
22. Taxay, Don. *History of the United States Mint and Coinage.* (New York: Sanford J. Durst, 1977).
23. http://eh.net/encyclopedia/article/whitten.panic.1893.
24. Ivy, Steve, and Ron Howard. *What Every Silver Dollar Buyer Should Know.* (Dallas: The Ivy Press, 1984), 80.
25. *Annual Report of the Director of the Mint,* 1897.
26. Yeoman, *Guide Book.*
27. *Coin Dealer Newsletter* (December 20, 1974). Reprinted in Q. David Bowers, *The Coin Dealer Newsletter: A Study in Rare Coin Price Performance 1964–1988.* (Wolfeboro, New Hampshire: Bowers and Merena Galleries, 1988).
28. Ivy and Howard, *Every Silver Dollar Buyer,* 107.
29. Yeoman, *Guide Book,* 30.
30. http://home.cc.umanitoba.
31. Ivy and Howard, *Every Silver Dollar Buyer,* 123.
32. Love, John. Personal recollection. Love's account also relayed by Bowers in *Silver Dollars and Trade Dollars.*
33. *Annual Report of the Director of the Mint,* 1902.
34. *Annual Report of the Director of the Mint,* 1903, 7.
35. Bowers, *Silver Dollars and Trade Dollars.*
36. Bureau of Labor Statistics, Consumer Price Index Inflation Calculator.
37. Yeoman, R.S. *A Guide Book of United States Coins.* (Racine, Wisconsin: 1962).
38. BLS, CPI Inflation Calculator.
39. Bowers, *Silver Dollars and Trade Dollars.*

Bibliography and Recommended Reading

Bowers, Q. David. *Encyclopedia of U.S. Paper Money*, Atlanta, GA, 2009.

— *A Guide Book of Morgan Silver Dollars* (4th ed.), Atlanta, GA, 2012.

— *Silver Dollars and Trade Dollars of the United States: A Complete Encyclopedia*, Wolfeboro, NH, 1993.

Breen, Walter. *Walter Breen's Complete Encyclopedia of U.S. and Colonial Coins*, New York, 1988.

Carothers, Neil. *Fractional Money: A History of Small Coins and Fractional Paper Currency of the United States* (Bowers and Merena ed.), 1990.

Crum, Adam, Oxman, Jeff, and Ungar, Selby. *Carson City Morgan Dollars* (3rd ed.), Atlanta, GA, 2014.

Doty, Richard. *America's Money, America's Story*, Atlanta, GA, 2008.

Fivaz, Bill, and Stanton, J.T. *Cherrypickers' Guide to Rare Die Varieties of United States Coins* (5th ed., vol. II), Atlanta, GA, 2012.

Haylings, George Wilfred. *The Profit March of Your Coin Investment: 1935–1971*, Manassas, VA, 1971.

Highfill, John. *The Comprehensive U.S. Silver Dollar Encyclopedia*, Broken Arrow, OK, 1992.

Ivy, Steve, and Howard, Ron. *What Every Silver Dollar Buyer Should Know*, Dallas, 1984.

Lange, David W. *History of the United States Mint and Its Coinage*, Atlanta, GA, 2005.

Lee, Karen M. *The Private Sketchbook of George T. Morgan, America's Silver Dollar Artist*, Atlanta, GA, 2013.

Mehl, B. Max. "The Most Extraordinary Collection of U.S. Large Cents. . . .", *The Numismatic Scrapbook Magazine*, August 20, 1959.

Miller, Wayne. *An Analysis of Morgan and Peace Dollars*, 1976.

Shafer, Neil. "The Morgan Silver Dollars, 1878–1921," *The Whitman Numismatic Journal*, Racine, WI, November 1964.

Taxay, Don. *History of the United States Mint and Coinage*, New York, 1977.

U.S. Mint. *Annual Report of the Director of the Mint*, Washington, D.C., various years.

Van Allen, Leroy C., and Mallis, A. George. *Comprehensive Catalogue and Encyclopedia of U.S. Morgan and Peace Silver Dollars*, New York, 1997.

Vermeule, Cornelius. *Numismatic Art in America: Aesthetics of the United States Coinage*, Atlanta, GA, 2007.

Yeoman, R.S. *A Guide Book of United States Coins*, Racine, WI, New York, NY, and Atlanta, GA, various editions.

About the Author

Michael "Miles" Standish is a professional numismatist specializing in United States and world coins. He was the first full-time coin grader at the Professional Coin Grading Service (PCGS), and currently serves as the firm's senior grader and vice president of business development.

Standish began his career in 1984, when American Numismatic Association executive director Edward C. Rochette hired him as an authenticator for the ANA Certification Service. Since then, working for PCGS, he has graded and authenticated hundreds of thousands of U.S. coins, including legends like the finest 1913 Liberty Head nickel, the "King of American Coins" (the 1804 dollar), and count-less of the finest Morgan dollars in private collections. He has championed the market for modern U.S. coins, developed innovative coin packaging concepts, advised dealers and hobbyists, presented expert testimony at trial, and mentored young numismatists. He spearheaded the development of limited-edition commemorative coin-and-autograph holders for former presidents Bush and Ford, Lance Armstrong, General Tommy Franks, Kathy Sullivan, Jessica Lynch, Nolan Ryan, and former U.S. Mint directors Donna Pope, Jay W. Johnson, Philip Diehl, and Edmund Moy. For his service to the hobby community and to the U.S. Mint, in 2011 Standish was awarded a "Director's Coin for Excellence" medal. He is the co-author, with retired Mint chief engraver John M. Mercanti, of *American Silver Eagles: A Guide to the U.S. Bullion Coin Program.*

Index

Index continued